I0510495

16 Pictures of the Bar

Ironic Mosaic of Legal World

Legal Stories 1.0, №1

Edited by Margarita Bokshtein

Moscow, 2019

Copyright 2019 by Margarita Bokshtein

All Rights Reserved. No part of this book may be reproduced in any manner without the express written consent of the publisher, except in the case of brief exerts in critical reviews or articles. All inquiries should be addressed to NAU LAB Publishing, stories@naulab.pro

NAU LAB Publishing books may be purchased in bulk at special discounts for sales promotion, corporate gifts, fundraising, or educational purposes. Special edition can also be created to specifications. For details, contact the Publishing Department at stories@naulab.pro

Editor's Preface

Human stories have always astonished me. Even more have I been attracted to what professionals have to say about the area they perform in. Nothing is as exciting to listen to than high class specialists telling good stories about cases, projects, mishappenings and hilarious characters of their world.

I have spent years collecting, writing down and spreading stories of my client lawyers. Considering the specific of legal profession, a witty and bright story is the easiest way to spread a word and initiate word-of-mouth promotion.

What surprised me for all these years was overall lack of full-size humorous storytelling in legal world. So, when I found these amazing worded pictures by Henry Wilcox I immediately knew, what was happening next.

Reading it comfortably in its original form was close to impossible. While editing this text we've learned how much the way we read and print has changed over the last century.

To be perfectly frank, my fellow lawyers found no real difference between what they see now and sketches from the book, so feel free to find your foes and friends in here.

This book was only the beginning. Then we reworked a book with sketches of the Bench and of the Jury and it turned into our series «LEGAL STORIES 1.0». I hope you enjoy this album of recognizable types and join us in our world call for stories

Margarita Bokshtein
Senior Partner of
NAU LAB business design laboratory

CHAPTER I. Functions

The proper function of a lawyer is to inform his client what his legal rights are and to assist him in obtaining those rights. This requires him to be a student of law, a seeker after truth, a champion of the right. It does not make him the accomplice of the thief, the pal of the highwayman, or the fence for a nest of criminals. If he divides spoils with pickpockets, shields assassins, or becomes a part of the burglars' tools, he does so in violation of his duty as a lawyer, he becomes such by yielding to the same corrupt purpose that inspires other criminals. Before the lawyer can correctly advise his client relative to his legal rights, he must become familiar with the facts that pertain thereto. Many facts must be garnered as a basis for the lawyer's opinion.

Usually the client is incompetent to collect these facts for he does not know exactly what material are and what immaterial, and someone having expert knowledge must act for him. In most cases the lawyer must discharge this duty, acting in conjunction with his client and employees.

This task should be performed with great accuracy, for on this depends the entire value of the lawyer's advice. In doing this the lawyer should seek only the truth. He should neither employ nor be deceived by liars. If he hunts for false testimony or becomes a loom for weaving lies to be sworn to by perjured witnesses, or counts upon his capacity to deceive or corrupt a judge or jury, he departs from the honorable task of a lawyer and becomes a public enemy.

Where the law is complicated many legal facts must be collected, such as the decisions of the courts of last resort, the latest Acts of the legislature, and such other authorities as are necessary to show the exact state of the law upon the subject. This work, also, must be done by the lawyer or his competent employees. His opinion will not be reliable unless these tasks are faithfully performed. The collection of legal facts is a tedious labor that can be mitigated only by a reverence for the law, a love of justice, and a high sense of professional duty.

The glutton, the gambler, and the drunkard are not liable to possess these qualities or engage in such a task to any extent. It is the bookworm who neglects the feast and the pursuit of the butterflies of sensual pleasure who is most likely to do this duty.

When the lawyer has gathered his stock of information he must act in a quasi-judicial capacity and decide for his client what are his legal rights. In performing this function, he has a more difficult task than the occupant of the bench, for he has not the advantage of hearing the questions discussed before him by trained advocates.

Also, he is quite likely to feel the deep interest which his client has in the controversy and partake of his desire to win, and thus possess a bias which clouds his judgment. He also has another task in forming a judgment which the judge does not have. After he has determined what is legal justice, he must decide upon the probability of being able to obtain it. A lawsuit is expensive and troublesome to the client even if he wins; and if he loses it is often a besom of destruction which may ruin him financially and fill his soul with sad regrets.

It is therefore very important that the lawyer should advise his client accurately as to the probability of success, for if he guides him into an unsuccessful suit he may be acquitted of moral blame, but he must stand convicted of having erred in his judgment. Having decided that his client has legal rights and that they probably can be obtained, the council must become an advocate, muster his forces, go before the court and fight to obtain these rights. The combat which he thus enters is often the fiercest of intellectual struggles. There is probably no contest where a larger number of mental faculties are called into use than in the conduct of a strongly contested lawsuit.

Let me refer to a few of these:

The first in importance is the memory. The advocate should be able to carry in mind all the details of his own forces, including the peculiar characteristics of his own client and witnesses and the exact facts that can be proven by their testimony, together with the plan which he has formed for the presentation of his evidence and legal authorities. He must have his proofs so arranged and in hand that he can present them with the greatest celerity, when necessary to strengthen his own position or weaken that of his adversary. He must set down in memory all that is said on his own side, all that is testified by his own witnesses and all that is presented by his adversary, so that he can quickly use this knowledge in forming a judgment as to the course to be pursued as the case proceeds. No lawyer ever had too good a memory, and one who can recollect accurately everything that occurs in the suit has one of the strongest weapons.

Next to memory is the power of perception. To be able to perceive quickly everything as soon as it happens, in precisely the way it happens, is a great faculty and of much use to the lawyer. It will also aid him greatly if he is able to perceive what things are about to happen or are likely to happen before they have actually occurred. This gives him more time to meet and parry the thrusts of his adversary.

Akin to perception is a sort of intuitive judgment of human nature, which he should have to enable him to sense the feelings of the witnesses, the judge, and the jury, and their tendencies, and thus avoid those things likely to produce prejudice or confusion, and to choose a method calculated to inspire confidence and a favorable consideration.

The faculty of speech is also important. It is well if the lawyer can express his views clearly, pleasantly, forcefully, fluently, naturally, and without affectation, in such a manner as to carry conviction. His manner, appearance, and entire conduct and bearing should be such as to win respect for his learning and integrity.

Courage is also demanded. If all due preparation has been made and everything which human foresight is able to suggest has been provided, the lawyer will still be subject to startling surprises. He will be disappointed by the weakness of his own forces and the strength of his adversary's; by the view which the Court takes of questions of law; by the mistakes and lapses of memory and stumbling of his witnesses, and by many other unexpected events beyond his control.

To endure this calmly requires a steady nerve and an unflinching determination, and where finally, as often happens, his well-laid plans, patient industry, and vigilant advocacy all terminate in defeat, and he must listen to the lament of his client and his client's family, and hear the cackling and crowing of the other side, and the numerous reasons why he was beaten, he certainly needs the strongest fiber of moral courage to remain undaunted and be able, without bias, fear, or false visions, to decide whether he will appeal the case to another tribunal or submit to the result.

If he decides to proceed further, he should still retain undiminished to the end of the case that unflagging zeal which he had at its inception, and a firm faith that if he does his best somehow and somewhere the right will surely prevail. Those demented by age or enfeebled by disease are hardly capable of such a task. The sluggard, the sportsman, the politician, and the inebriate will never seriously attempt it. To be a real lawyer, capable and thorough, leaves but small room for sidestepping.

That the lawyer seldom possesses all the faculties above referred to, fully developed, we must all admit. That there is wide room for improvement in the profession all concede. To point out some of the many shortcomings ought to be beneficial to the profession and public generally, and this I will now attempt.

[10]

CHAPTER II. Verbosity

The notion prevails that a lawyer should be a fluent talker, that he should have the "gift of gab." A ready and terse utterance is certainly desirable, but it frequently happens this talent is developed to such excess as to become a source of weakness. A law of physics applies here. The force which can be expended in any given time is limited and that portion exerted in one act cannot be retained for another.

There may be some who have such a superabundance of physical and mental energy as to be capable of a large variety of actions at the same time and be able to continue such actions for many hours without repose, but I have no such person in mind. All excessive talkers known to me have slighted their tasks and could not be safely relied upon to do work requiring much skill and accuracy in its execution. All voluntary motions of the mind and body require attention, and the expense of force, and force expended is lost. This applies with great emphasis to the practice of the law.

Colonel Bombast

Colonel Bombast was a verbose lawyer. From youth he had shown such fluency of utterance, took such delight in talking, became so zealous and enthusiastic while thus engaged, had such a vocabulary of words on the end of his tongue, was so ready with illustrations, quotations, and epigrammatic expressions, that everyone who knew him prophesied for him a great career.

At sociables, clubs, and many public and private gatherings he was the center of an admiring throng, where he stood or sat with his thumbs in his vest holes and with his head thrown back, shaking vigorously, as he poured forth a perpetual torrent of words. At banquets, celebrations, receptions, or other public occasions where there was a program or an address of welcome, a toast or eulogy, he was in demand. All who heard him wondered at the exuberance of his metaphors, the brilliancy of his wit, and the extent of his vocabulary. He was called "silver-tongued," "golden-throated," "the modern Demosthenes," and other appellations of a similar import.

The slightest suggestion was sufficient to excite in his mind the most gorgeous images. If a drop of water were mentioned he thought of all forms of water from the roaring ocean to the rolling thunder cloud, from the ice rattling in the glass to the iceberg floating in the polar sea, from the dropping tear to the raging Niagara. If a wing was mentioned there flitted before his mind all kinds of winged creatures from the microscopic insect to the largest bird. The word flower opened up before his mind's eye in panoramic splendor every blossom that he had ever beheld.

Nor was this all. His nimble fancy collected the component parts of all things of which he had seen, read, or heard, and formed new images of things which had never existed. The thought of a bug suggested to him a bug as large as an elephant; a grain of gold, a gold mountain; a small diamond, a great planet composed of the same substance. The bright places of the heavens were radiant with myriads of angels, and the dark spots of earth inhabited by frightful demons. The visions that thus came trooping before his mind often had little or no connection with each other. He soon lost the subject under discussion, and no one could predict from his beginning where he would end.

Those who met him for the first time found him very delightful, but after an extended acquaintance his excessive mouthings became so irksome that it is said even his wife took refuge in "solitaire" to avoid conversing with him, and his friends often crossed the street to escape meeting him. There is a limit to human knowledge, and usually a narrow limit to the knowledge of great talkers. They can only keep their vocal organs in operation by repetitions, and when one has heard their stock of ideas, he loses interest. So, it was with Colonel Bombast. If you suggested that it was a pleasant day he would forthwith begin a disquisition upon the weather, carry you all over the world, and tell you over and over again the eminent people with whom he had an intimate association and connect them with the subject by telling what he had said to them and they had said to him about the weather. If you gave him time, he would weave in all the history of his life, the great speeches he had made and those he was about to make.

When he was admitted to the bar many prophesied that he would become a great lawyer. Did they expect such a genius would examine critically the technicalities of the law and search among the roots of its doctrines to become familiar with their obscure origins, that he would deny himself the pleasure of talking to commune with the statutes and constitutions of his state and his nation, and the efforts that have been made from time to time by the courts to construe them? Would he be likely to scurry out at night to unfrequented localities, visit the hovels of wretchedness and interview their miserable occupants for the purpose of getting evidence to be used in a suit? Would he explore scientific books for the meaning of terms and procure the latest information relative to matters in a legal controversy?

On the contrary, would he not set his sails to catch the sweetest zephyrs, and steer his easy sailing bark over the gentlest waters? And so he did. The ignorant public attracted by his mellifluous utterances trusted him with their cases. He assured them in boastful phrases that they were sure to win, and they believed him until, finally, as was usually the case, they met with disaster. Then he accounted for the result by charging the judge and jury with imbecility or corruption.

Occasionally, however, he won, and when he did, he advertised the fact, exaggerated the importance of the victory, and thus spread the impression that he was a successful lawyer.

Many people and some that have much money are easily induced to buy a gold brick, and such judge of a lawyer by his bloviating assurances and the amount of noise he can stir up in the community. Colonel Bombast never lacked patronage. His addresses abounded in the usual stock illustrations common to excessive talkers.

In a speech delivered in defense of a tramp who had stolen a hand sled, he referred to the Fall of Rome, the Goddess of

Liberty, Christ before Pilate, a storm at sea, and the burning of Servetus by John Calvin. He spoke of "God's green earth" many times, often appealed to the jury in the name of heaven and wound up with the "Sermon on the Mount."

He used the same references in a speech to recover damages from a butcher for selling tainted meat. In this address he began with the "Sermon on the Mount" and finished with the "Fall of Rome," which fall he attributed to the degeneration caused by tainted meat.

Likewise, when defending a corporation for tapping a water pipe and stealing water from the city, he indulged in the same startling illustrations and closed with Christ's forgiveness of the erring woman as a reason why the jury should be merciful to the purloiner of the city water. These few well-known subjects of rhetoric were usually woven into his addresses, but were of course treated with variations and clothed at times with slightly different words, but in speeches of considerable length he generally managed to make them fit and do effective duty.

He was also addicted to alliteration. On one occasion while striving to exalt the credibility of one of his witnesses in comparison with the witness of his adversary he said:

"The dull, dumb-headed dunce who testified on the opposite side can no more be compared with my intelligent witness than the puny pinhead of a Pawnee chief with the ponderous pate of a Roman emperor, or the faint flickerings of the firefly with the scorching scintillations of the summer sun."

When trying to humble the pride of a certain individual, he said:

"Gentlemen of the Jury, who is this addlepated ass with the ossified spine? I can tell you. When I came to this country, he was tramping jimson weeds and pulling cockleburs from his whiskers. He was then as poor as dishwater, and the wind whistled mournfully through his breeches. Then he was as meek as Moses and glad to fleece the stones for forage and be decent. Now look at him. Because an inscrutable Providence has removed him thirty days from the poorhouse, he struts like a turkeycock with the rickets, and assumes to give orders to God Almighty."

His grandiloquent periods sometimes became ill placed. On one occasion he defended a railroad company for killing a farmer's cow. The farmer's lawyer offered the rules of the railroad to show that the train when it struck the cow was exceeding the speed provided in these rules. The Colonel arose with his usual magnificent air and after several caressing twists of the portentous blue-black mustache that clouded a large part of his countenance, he treated the court to the following:

[18]

"Your Honor, the defendant objects. It, sir, has been a question from time immemorial down to the present day with our wisest sages as to whether the Almighty Ruler of the Universe has endowed dumb brutes with capacity to reason. The matchless minds of ancient Athens pondered in vain over this perplexing problem. The intellectual giants of the middle ages tumbled into their tombs and left it still unsolved, and I believe, sir, it is an unsettled question yet. The rules and regulations of the railroad could not benefit this cow, for, sir, it has not yet been shown that she could read and understand these regulations."

In the trial of his cases the Colonel was a terror to both court and jury, and it frequently happened he talked a good case to defeat. The human tongue is a nice instrument which to be used effectively must be handled with care. Every idle word is a waste. The person who must do much talking must devote much time to reading and reflection, or his speeches will become stale and tiresome. This applies with great force to the practice of law.

***

The common blatherskite may sit on a dry goods box on the sunny side of a country store or wear out an arm chair in a hotel lobby and talk fluently relative to what the law ought to be and assume to know much about what the law really is, but the lawyer must examine statutes and constitutions and read extensively from reported cases before he is able to speak above a whisper on the subject, and then his words are likely to be very precise and guarded.

The general public should beware of the verbose lawyer who, like an overloaded bag of wind, is perpetually blurting out opinions upon every question. The man who finds his chief delight in listening to his own voice should seek some other occupation where the rights, liberties, and estates of mankind are not put in such jeopardy as they are when entrusted to the victim of this peculiar vice.

CHAPTER III. Sociability

EXTENSIVE reading is required to learn the law and keep informed of its frequent changes. Much study and reflection are necessary in planning for legal contests. These require seclusion and the shutting out of the diverting and enticing influences of society. The young man who has no taste for solitude and is unhappy when not enjoying the society of his fellows should not undertake the duties of this profession. In the country it may be easier to obtain and endure solitude, but in the cities the opportunities for entertainment and the allurements of pleasure are so numerous it is very difficult for one who craves such luxuries to suffer the self-denial. The number of those who have failed to do this is so great and the need of it so apparent that illustration is hardly necessary. But I will introduce

BILLIE GOODFELLOW

He was one of the brightest and best mixers. In his youth it was "Hurrah, boys," to the apple orchard, the melon patch, or the swimming hole. When any scheme of pleasure was proposed he was ready to take part. As he grew up, he learned all the social games, took an eager interest in all sports and found time to go with everybody. He was always in great demand. He could mingle with any grade of intelligence, fellowship with any moral status, and accommodate himself as easily as water to any strata. The servant girl, the bootblack, or the society queen, all were Billie's friends and liked to entertain him and be entertained by him. He was at home at a labor picnic, a church fair, a political or ministerial association. He was as popular in a Sunday school class as in a saloon. Wherever he went he became the center around which the delighted multitude clustered like swarming bees.

He was most happy when those around him were most hilarious and frivolous. His presence was a perpetual fountain of joy. His face was rosy with bounding blood, his body short and fat. His hair curly and his brown eyes twinkled with merriment. The corners of his mouth turned up like a god of mirth's, and his countenance beamed with ecstatic delight while luxuriating in the society of his friends. He seemed designed by nature to call mankind from their cares and sorrows and invite them to come with him to the feast and pleasure grounds.

Originally Billie had inherited some money, but he parted with it easily, and after it was gone his gay life was maintained by foraging upon his friends. When he had anything he could lend, anyone could borrow it, and thus he became a kind of middleman, borrowing from the rich and lending to the poor. He had no prejudice against paying his debts, and perhaps did so when he found it convenient, but ordinarily it was not. No one can accommodate himself to all classes without being a neat and graceful liar and an expert peddler of false promises. In this particular Billie had talent. It was as natural for him to deceive as it is for the little potato bug when approached to curl in its legs, roll onto its back and pretend to be dead. It was a real pleasure to hear him lie. He did it in such a sincere and sanctimonious manner, and when caught at it smiled so sweetly and slid out of it so smoothly that no one was jarred by discovering the prevarication.

Men of his character often try to entertain by sallies of wit, smart retorts, and the telling of funny stories. This is a precarious method, for wit loses its edge when much employed, and funny stories seem ridiculous to many. Billie chose a more direct method of amusing people. He was an appreciative listener, laughed heartily at the jokes of others, bestowed praise at every opportunity, and inspired those about him to an exalted opinion of themselves. He was like a glass into which they could look and see their images glorified. Many were grateful for this service and felt a warm friendship for him. They forgave his peculiar financial habits and neglect of truth and were pleased to strew flowers in his path wherever he went.

His charming manners assisted in obtaining credit and in beating his creditors. He was indebted to a tailor for a suit of clothes and had so often ignored his request for payment that the tailor's patience became exhausted and he gave the claim to a collection lawyer. This collection lawyer called at Billie's office to demand payment.

When he came in Billie grasped him by the hand cordially, expressed great delight in seeing him, gave him a good cigar and a glass of wine, offered him the use of his library and the freedom of his office, treated the visit as a friendly call and chided him for not sooner calling, and expressed a wish to render the collector all assistance in his power for advancement in the legal profession. He also introduced him to his associates and others in his office. He entertained the collector so royally that he left without presenting the bill and returned it to the tailor, stating that he did not wish to take the case.

The disgusted tailor then grabbed the bill, and without waiting to put on his coat started for Billie 's office. There he learned Billie had gone home. With zeal still unabated he went straightway to Billie's residence, determined to make his recreant debtor discharge his obligation. Billie met him at the door with an appearance of great delight, ushered him into his luxurious parlor, introduced him to his charming wife and daughter and insisted upon his drinking a glass of wine and staying to supper. He sent out for some of his neighbors to come in and provided the tailor with a coat to wear at the impromptu reception. He commended the tailor very highly as a gentleman and a scholar, and treated him with such affectionate regard that it seemed out of place for the tailor to mention the claim that he had come to collect, and he left without asking for his account but not until Billie had succeeded in getting a temporary loan from him of fifteen dollars.

Such a man as Billie Goodfellow rarely finds time to learn the indices to a law library, and how he got his license no one knew. It is probable that the favorable breeze that had fanned him in other pursuits filled his sails and gave his light bark an easy sailing into the legal harbor. Occasionally he won a case. Courts and juries sometimes warped the law and construed the evidence in favor of his client so as to give Billie the victory. Sometimes the opposing counsel settled with Billie out of a desire to aid him.

He was able by his peculiar, ingenious methods to wiggle many persons out of difficulty. A man was indicted in five counts charged with forging five checks. He first employed a skilled technical lawyer. After a long and unsuccessful legal battle over the form and sufficiency of the indictment, this lawyer, having no doubt of the prisoner's guilt, gave up the case as hopeless.

Then the accused sent for Billie. Billie learned that the prisoner had a handsome wife and a young baby. These he took to the prosecuting attorney and finally persuaded that official to accept a plea of guilty on one charge of forgery and dismiss the others. He then took the wife and baby to the judge who was to pronounce the sentence and worked on his feelings. The judge might have sentenced the prisoner to the penitentiary for ten years, but he fixed the term at six months.

Billie then visited the sheriff with these two objects of sympathy, and this official agreed to delay taking the culprit to the penitentiary for two days. Billie then took his aids to the office of a friendly physician and had him visit the prisoner and make affidavit that he found him afflicted with "Bright's Disease," and that incarceration in the penitentiary would probably hasten his death. With this affidavit and the wife and baby Billie went to his friend the Governor and made such a moving plea that his excellency granted a pardon and the prisoner was freed.

A large, healthy-looking woman who had two small children was arrested for selling liquor in violation of law. Ten different offences were charged against her. She employed a lawyer who was a noted orator to try her first case. She came into court dressed in a sealskin cloak, with her fingers and ears ornamented with gems. She was painted and powdered and looked like the "woman of Babylon." All that the orator could say did not save her. A jury of pronounced prohibitionists gathered by the constable for the purpose promptly convicted her, and she appealed the case. This orator considered it useless to try the other cases and asked to be released from the task.

Then Billie was employed. He got a continuance of the case, told the woman to move out to a suburb of the city, rent a shanty and put out a sign, "Washing Done Here," and when she came to court to appear as a washerwoman, unvarnished and dressed in clean but plain apparel, and bring her children with her. This she did. The prosecution proved that she had sold a glass of liquor to a decoy sent out by the Temperance Society. The jury were prohibitionists selected from the crank row, but they were good men who were impressed by the honest and poverty-stricken appearance of this mother and her innocent little children clinging to her.

Billie 's speech was short. He merely said: "My dear friends, I do not think our noble cause of temperance will be benefited by taking these children from their mother and thrusting her into prison where she can earn no money to support them. But I leave the matter to you with the understanding that if you convict her you and my friend the prosecuting attorney will join me in making up a purse to support these poor children while their mother languishes in prison." The children and mother both began crying, the prosecuting attorney made no answer, and the jury retired and returned with a verdict of "Not guilty," and the other cases against her were dismissed.

A man, very offensive, who had just returned from serving a term in the penitentiary, was indicted on the complaint of a bright little girl of twelve years for a criminal assault upon her. The public indignation was so great against the prisoner that there was danger of lynching, and he had difficulty to get any attorney to undertake his defense. Finally, he convinced Billie that he was innocent and that the child had been induced by her parents, who were his enemies, to make this infamous charge. By offering prizes for new pupils, Billie succeeded in getting the little girl to become a member of his Sunday school class, and when the case came on for trial an enormous crowd, eager for the punishment of the accused, were treated to a surprise. The child was put upon the witness stand and questioned by the prosecuting attorney, and, to the astonishment of all but Billie, she contradicted her story before the grand jury and swore that the defendant was innocent, and the court ordered his acquittal.

In another case a man was indicted for horse stealing. His guilt was evident, but he was poor and had a large family, and Billie undertook his defense. He ascertained that the thief had a sister who was a soldier's widow and lived in a little cottage on a small farm which her husband had left her. He got one of his friends, who was called a bail shark, to go on the bail bond of the accused and take as security a mortgage on the widow's homestead. Then when the thief was out of jail he disappeared and could not be found, the bail shark was about to settle the bond and foreclose his mortgage, and thus the widow would be made homeless. Billie saw some old soldier friends of his and they brought the matter to the attention of the Grand Army of the Republic, and this association, to save the widow's homestead, influenced the Governor to remit the forfeiture of the bond.

***

Many similar instances could be related showing the methods by which Billie's clients often profited by his services, but none will contend he was a real lawyer. He was incompetent to advise on any abstruse law point or to make an argument on any difficult legal question. While he might sometimes cause Justice to break her sword, he rarely rendered the blind goddess any assistance in solving her difficult problems.

CHAPTER IV.
The Literary Lawyer

MEMBERS of the legal profession are often enamored by the charms of literature. The student is early exposed to fascinating books, and those which give him the most pleasure ordinarily receive the most attention. There may be youths who yearn for scientific facts and statistics and take intense delight in searching for the actual and the positive, but their minds usually prefer the highly colored exaggerations of fancy to the real facts of everyday life and the tested truths of science. It has never been considered vicious to indulge a taste for literature, and many members of the legal profession have taken

pride in their excellence in this respect.

Reginald Writer

is presented as a type of the literary lawyer. He had fine red hair, a full freckled face, was small in stature and neatly constructed. He allowed his shining locks to grow long, pass in graceful waves over his noble brow, and behind his small ears, and then fall upon his bronzed neck. He had no filthy habits; took no interest in sports or games of chance; considered ordinary society stupid and sought only the company of the refined and literary. These were usually the delicate sex. He could recite many pages from works of famous English poets and quote liberally from poets in other languages.

He could recall verses appropriate to any subject suggested. He was happiest when surrounded by admiring friends who were listening and commenting on his exquisite taste and marvelous memory. Nor was he content with quotations. He spent many days and nights in framing, smoothing out, and stringing together effusions of his own. By unusual words linked with classic references he expressed the usual feelings that animated him and read these to his pretended admirers, who would listen and try to look pleased. But poetry was not his only ambition. He became familiar with the most prominent fiction writers, ancient and modern.

He obtained and read the latest novels by the best authors, determined that no one should speak of a new book in his presence and compel him to be dumb. His eyelids were often red with excessive reading, and a hacking cough told of weak lungs acquired in the same way. His mind collected and stored away the cream of all he read, and he could quickly present a delicious mixture on any subject whenever he desired.

Consequently, his society was eagerly sought for, and wherever he appeared multitudes gathered to enjoy the delightful droppings from his tongue. But literature was not his profession. He offered his services to the public as a lawyer. He had a beautiful office. Its walls were ornamented with portraits. Its niches were made attractive by busts. But they were not portraits or busts of prominent lawyers. Richly carved bookcases contained many splendidly bound books, but they were not statutes or treatises upon law. His speeches in court were models of rhetoric, but they were not encumbered with citations from legal treatises or reports. When his case terminated unfavorably his description of the stupidity and depravity of the judge and jury was in elegant diction.

It was a pleasure to hear his clear, sweet voice and brilliant sentences either when talking to the court or jury or in talking about them. All conceded that Reginald was a rare gentleman and a scholar, who added grace and dignity to his profession. Few stopped to inquire what proportion of his cases ended disastrously, or to note that in the learning of his profession he was in fact an ignoramus. Charmed by his manners and his eloquence, his clients were unable to see why they were not wise in selecting him as their lawyer. Thus, upon the altar of literary excellence the rights of many were sacrificed.

The literary lawyer is sometimes required to speak on a theme not adapted to the delicate tracery of his style. Then his liquid lines appear grotesque. As an illustration take Reginald's great speech in the

"Scratch Case."

Miss Mehitable Scratch was a maiden lady who had an inordinate love for a bull pug. To provide milk for her dear dog it was claimed that she infracted "the statutes in such cases made and provided" by clandestinely catching and milking a nannie goat belonging to Zabriskie Slobelobsky. The owner of the goat had her arrested for stealing milk, and Reginald was employed to defend her. His speech cannot be inserted in full, and these extracts give an inadequate idea of its excellence:

"The saffron morn," he said, "overspread the orient with rosy blushes when this tender maid tripped forth on her loving errand. Her light and gentle foot scarcely brushed the dew that bejeweled the verdant lawn as she flew like a bird to the home of this solitary goat. Little recked she that this benevolent animal, with udders swelling with the nourishing nectar, had an owner, with heart so flinty and soul so sordid, as to deny to her beloved canine the juice so necessary to its life.

Had she so opined she might have chosen instead midnight's dun and dreadful hour, when the depraved Slobelobsky was enchained in rancid dreams and her visit would have been hid in sweet oblivion. But love, unselfish, overwhelming love, that bursts the bud of every noble purpose, so filled her with its thrill that she thought only of her cherished pet, her faithful, mild-eyed, ever-constant pug, whose thirsty throat was parching for the milk this whiskered goat so readily could yield.

Meanwhile, this Slobelobsky lay in wait, guarding his goat with jealous eye, deaf to the hungry whinings of the noble pug, hoarding its milk as misers do their gold, perceived her soft approach, and ere she had drawn forth a dozen drops, thwarted her holy purpose, nabbed her, and dragged her from his goat, and now seeks her undoing. Thinks he a jury have no hearts to feel the dint of pity, that they are blind to maiden's modest love. This pug was all she had to call her own. Her heart's pure love was centered on her pug. The pangs of hunger that he felt pierced to her inmost soul. Her nightly prayers to heaven were for her pet — that every breeze should fan him lightly and bathe him in the balm of many blossoms.

Could she see Slobelobsky's goat overcharged with milk, until its creamy fluid dripped useless on the ground, and take no steps to slake her famished pug? Oh, ye immortal gods! It was not possible. True, Slobelobsky owned the goat, and, technically, could claim its milk, but what are barren technicalities when fencing 'against the pangs of hunger? Mere webs of gossamer that float upon the summer air. It was said by Avon's mighty bard; 'The quality of mercy is not strained, it drops like the gentle dew from heaven upon the place beneath" etc.

Then proceeding to the end with the familiar quotation he closed with a piteous plea for mercy for the fond Mehitabel. His opponent was not an orator. He merely suggested that this light-footed maiden, should not be so light fingered. That she should love justice more and pug dogs less and not rob Slobelobsky's children of their needed milk to make wrinkles on this wall-eyed lump of lazy fat.

He admitted that the quality of mercy was not strained, and neither was the goat's milk. But it did not drop like the gentle dew from heaven but was extracted from the fodder Slobelobsky's hands had provided. No amount of misdirected affection for this bunch of adipose tissue was an excuse for stealing milk. The misguided maiden was convicted but her sentence was light.

It was usually on such flights of rhetoric that Reginald relied and sometimes they were effective but usually they were avoided by points of law which he was not prepared to discuss or did not understand. The time was when law books were so few and legal principles so scant and unsettled that a lawyer could successfully devote a great part of his time to general reading and achieve the highest success at the bar.

***

But now so great has become the number of established legal principles and so numerous the decisions that qualify them, so varied and complex the statutes and ordinances that relate to them and so technical the rules of practice, that an extensive knowledge of law books is indispensable. There is also an ever-increasing domain of scientific knowledge, which is intimately connected with the facts involved in most lawsuits. Success depends more upon close examination and an accurate perception of facts and legal principles than upon feelings and fancies.

The lawyer who now devotes much time to far-fetched works of the imagination is likely to be but poorly equipped for his task. He may to some extent revel in the delights of literature and yet do satisfactory legal work, but he must not drift too far from shore or fly too high above the solid ground.

CHAPTER V. The Desire for Office

PROBABLY every male citizen of the United States has felt at some time a desire to occupy an official position. To hold office is believed to be glorious even though nothing is added to the character or quality of the individual thereby. So well-nigh universal is this belief that no office however meager its functions, is without a charm that attracts many competing candidates. Even the opportunity to guard the outside door of a voluntary association is sufficient to attract numerous aspirants and the one elected feels exalted and is exalted in the eyes of his fellows.

The notion that an officer is a superior being is a survival of monarchy, wherein the King claimed to be God's anointed, and those who held official positions under him were considered as indirectly selected by Deity on account of their particular fitness to discharge a divine function. We reject the doctrine of the Divine right of kings, but we have coined the phrase "The voice of the people is the voice of God" and thus set up a fetish of the same nature. The most desirable position for the individual would seem to be the one where the largest compensation is paid for the least labor, care and responsibility, and where the highest degree of personal liberty is permitted.

Most offices are in this respect undesirable; the occupant being the servant of several masters and clothed with heavy responsibilities. The number of such masters and the weight of responsibilities usually increase as the importance of the office increases, so that in the highest offices the occupant has but small time for rest, little liberty of action, scant privacy, and is so loaded with responsibility that he has no peace and his principal enjoyment is that small satisfaction which an ambitious egoist takes in giving orders and in occupying a conspicuous place. But no amount of wisdom is sufficient to protect the average man against this craving for public office, and the lawyer is no exception.

From early infancy his ears have been filled with the prophecies of doting parents and admiring friends predicting for him the highest places in the country. Many of the books he has read tell of young lawyers who have thus won deathless fame. Every newspaper either directly or indirectly exalts and glorifies persons in official positions.

When an occasion has required an orator to address the public some prominent official has usually been selected even though known to be the dullest and weariest of speakers. A tongue-tied public officer has been preferred to a real orator who occupied no official position. When great cases have occurred attracting wide attention and justified the payment of large fees his foolish neighbors have gone far to procure the services of some prominent public official or ex-public official, who has had small learning and less experience in the law and this only as incidents to his political experience, preferring him to the expert lawyer who has never sought or held a public office. These facts turn the heads of ambitious young lawyers in the direction of politics to the injury of the legal profession.

There was a time in the history of this government, when the domain of knowledge necessary to be covered by members of the bar was not so large as to prevent a concurrent practice of politics. But so greatly has this domain now expanded that an expert lawyer is allowed no time for outside exploits. Meanwhile the practice of politics has become a profession requiring for its successful pursuit all the time and energies of which any person is capable. The politician has no period when he can carefully pursue legal studies or consider legal propositions. The lawyer who tries to practice politics and the politician who attempts to practice law are not likely to meet with any real success in either profession.

Such may use the legal profession as a cover for dirty political work or may use the profession of politics as an excuse for doing corrupt and unprofessional legal work, and may make money by the twin devices. The same person will rarely become a thorough politician in the highest sense and an expert and honorable lawyer. Many good persons however have thought otherwise and have faithfully tried to serve the two mistresses. There are different channels by which young lawyers may thus be led astray. Let me here illustrate.

Lawrence Lobby

Lawrence Lobby was by nature fitted to take high rank in the law. He had a broad, noble brow, large sparkling blue eyes, a Byronic mouth and classical nose; was tall, straight and well proportioned, and unusually graceful in his motions. He possessed remarkable fluency in language, a retentive memory and a keen and discriminating intelligence. Many who saw him and heard him speak pronounced him a man that nature had fashioned especially for the law.

By energy, economy and close attention to his studies he graduated with honors both in the classical and law departments of one of the best universities and was at once welcomed into a prominent law firm where he found a fine library, competent assistants and advisers to aid him, and clients waiting to employ his services. The firm which he had entered did a large corporation business and had many clients engaged in interstate commerce. These were often made victims of unfavorable legislation by the State Legislatures and the National Congress and were frequently put in much trepidation by threats of such legislation.

It seemed as if these bodies soon after assembling had selected the corporations vulnerable to such assaults and had prepared and referred to committees' bills calculated to frighten these corporations into making strenuous efforts to prevent vicious legislation. This made a demand for what is known as a political department and the suavity, grace and fine address, of young Lobby, were soon utilized for the purpose of conducting this political department. It was not long before he found himself mired neck-deep in politics.

It was his duty to become acquainted with politicians and public officers, to organize and manipulate machines, to 'conduct banquets, special excursions and arrange tours for the purpose of cultivating the acquaintance and winning the favor of legislators, members of Congress, judges and other officials. He became a distributor of railroad passes, gifts, and other special favors, the chief center of a sphere of influence which covered a wide area. He held many interviews by day and attended many functions at night. He soon got "in the swim," became one of the charmed circle and was conspicuous in the public eye as one of the political darlings of the nation.

He was at home in the society of the wealthy and a graceful courtier at the feet of the very rich. He indulged in all luxuries, reared his children in an atmosphere of splendor, accumulated much wealth and was widely known. He pretended to be a lawyer and was sometimes employed to act as one in important cases, but his principal services were in the line of politics. The political influence he had thus acquired made him especially valuable in procuring and preventing legislation. Take a few samples of his efforts in this respect.

It was learned that heirs to a large estate were intending to contest the will. The existing law allowed two years after the death of the testator to begin such proceedings. One year had been permitted to elapse without bringing suit, and Lawrence Lobby was employed to defend against the threatened contest. He induced the Legislature to amend the law so as to allow but one year after the death to bring the suit in such a case. The contest was prevented.

Another method he employed in defending a suit was to get the Legislature to repeal the law giving the right of action after the suit was begun. His methods of preventing legislation were to induce the member having charge of the bill to delay or withdraw it, or perhaps procure some clerk to steal and secrete it when too late to substitute another. Sometimes he frightened the member urging its passage by getting many of his influential constituents to sign a protest against the bill. Sometimes both methods were employed. He was especially useful in getting the allowance of claims by Congress or the State Legislature. These claims were usually apocryphal. Take a few instances:

Suppose that General Washington, on his way to New York to be inaugurated President of the United States had met with an accident; that his horse had been lamed and he had borrowed one from a farmer and had failed to return it. Suppose the descendants of this farmer now make a claim against the United States for the value of this horse and interest thereon. Lawrence Lobby here would be useful.

Of course, he would claim that the animal was of remarkably rare breed and that his value with interest would amount to many thousand dollars. Or suppose when General Washington was crossing the Delaware to capture the Hessians he had used boats belonging to a Navigation Company and failed to take good care of them and to pay either for the damage done or for the use of the boats. The claim that Lobby would make against the Government with accumulated interest would amount to a colossal sum.

Or suppose that when the battle of Bunker Hill was fought, some of the brave Continentals had run over a bean-patch belonging to a Boston gardener, and the descendants of the owner of this bean-patch had employed Lobby to recover damages, he would certainly have claimed that there had been the destruction of the finest collection of green beans that Boston ever knew. The alleged value of the vegetables thus destroyed would be prodigious, and the interest since accumulated thereon amount to enough to make even a billion-dollar Congress pause.

Who would be so unpatriotic as to oppose the payment of such claims? What worthy descendant of our brave sires would dishonor their names by repudiating the obligations they had thus contracted. The Government then so poor, and now gorged with wealth, it would be claimed could well afford to reward with lavish hand the heirs of the original creditors, for the patient waiting of their ancestors.

The fine features and persuasive voice of Lawrence Lobby were especially useful in refreshing such stale claims. Thus, his splendid intellect capable of rendering such valuable service to his country was perverted into channels for corrupting the public morals and despoiling multitudes of his fellow citizens. He had his day of seeming triumph, but he felt not the satisfaction that comes to an upright and skillful lawyer in the honorable discharge of the duties of his profession. The fawning crowd that profited by aiding him in his nefarious schemes and even his corrupt employers really despised him on account of the character of his services.

CHAPTER VI. Desire for Office, Continued

Peter Protest

TAKE another example of a lawyer led astray by politics.

Peter Protest was awkward and ungainly in appearance, had stooped shoulders, sunken eyes, beetling eyebrows, high cheek bones, large jointed hands, unusually large feet, a crooked neck, an irregular and slanting mouth, and a dark, bilious complexion. But what nature had denied him in personal charms she had made up to him in mental and spiritual unfoldment. He early evinced a taste for learning. He eschewed all games and resisted the allurements of pleasure. His companions were his books. When he became a man, he chose the legal profession and by steady diligence filled his retentive memory with the general principles of jurisprudence.

Without aid from the schools he became able to try with unusual skill such cases as come to a young lawyer. His success rapidly advertised his talents. His services were sought by many clients willing to pay liberally and he might have become a great lawyer but for this: Early in life he had felt the injustice apparent in human society and noted the unequal distribution of the earnings of labor. His kind heart and courageous nature prompted him to strive for a remedy. This is a noble ambition and when it has once entered the soul it takes such root that all else must yield to its indulgence.

Animated by this spirit he entered politics where he championed the cause of the weak and wretched against the prosperous and powerful. He became the leader of an awkward squad, poorly organized, rent with dissensions, full of distress, loaded with grievances, but very numerous and determined to change if possible the social conditions. These were opposed by a host thoroughly organized, well provisioned, proud, self-complacent, strongly entrenched and provided with the most effective weapons.

He was usually defeated in his political efforts but thereby he became more firmly convinced of the justice of his cause, the depravity of his adversaries and the stronger in his determination to sacrifice himself for its benefit. He tightened up his armor with undiminished zeal for another combat. Yet he sought employment as a lawyer and took cases of the most important character.

After he became fully identified with the cause of the oppressed his clients were mostly the poor and he was of course unable to give but slight attention to their matters. His practice covered a wide range and as the poor man's lawyer there came to him a great variety of damage claims to be collected on shares. The notoriety he had acquired in politics brought to him the halt, the crippled and the feeble-minded of both sexes. He was often made the victim of misplaced confidence. His poverty-stricken clients for whom he had toiled diligently in prosecuting suits frequently settled behind his back and for his share of the fruits gave him the icy stare.

The miserable rascals he had worked so hard to defend usually made no effort to pay him and while he was congratulating one of them on his acquittal the culprit stole his watch. He secured the release of a client charged with murder on the ground that he was insane at the time he did the killing. When Protest had to sue on the contract for his pay, the assassin plead insanity to avoid the contract. With much sympathy and zeal, he prosecuted a claim for damages made by a woman against a preacher for kissing her and after the case was ended, she paid Protest for his services by suing him for a breach of promise.

[50]

When fifty members of the miner's Committee were arrested in mid-winter by a combination of coal companies to suppress a strike, he contributed from his own funds to fill the empty coal boxes and scanty cupboards around which their poor families shivered while husbands and fathers were in jail; he went before the court and by his eloquence secured their acquittal, charged nothing and paid his own expenses.

The following Autumn when he was running for the Legislature against the attorney who had tried the case against this committee, they furnished the votes to defeat Protest, although he was the regular candidate on the labor ticket. In the fumes of liquor purchased for them by his opponent all recollection of obligation to him was quenched. In a city where 50,000 laboring men strained their throats cheering for him as a candidate, he got less than 500 votes.

While making an earnest plea for justice for the poor before an audience of his constituents one of them stole his overcoat. But these were trifles. He was seldom appreciated by the poor or understood by the rich. The silk tiles and ostrich plumes nodded scornfully and passed by on the other side. The wool hats and straw bonnets treated him with complacent contempt. The champions of vested interests dubbed him a demagogue and the unthinking considered him a crank. But he toiled on cultivating the stony land of self-sacrifice, pierced by the shafts of malice, torn by the briers of ingratitude, waiting for scant justice in an epitaph, or a reward in heaven.

His ears were filled with cries of distress, his eyes were assailed by spectacles of squalor, above him the threatening heavens lowered tempestuously and about him the ocean of human passions raged furiously. He had no chart, no compass and no guide, except a pale star seen only by faith through impenetrable clouds, the feeble hope that when he had done his best somehow and sometime justice would come.

How could a person so situated find time to carefully prepare for the trial of a lawsuit or the seclusion to analyze cases and observe the nice distinctions made by the courts? Yet he did make the attempt and won some cases; but great were the losses sustained by many of his admirers who employed him to represent them in court. The multitude of his engagements caused many delays and continuances and when finally, he got a furlough from the political army long enough to try a case he had made no preparation and his mind was in a nebulous condition unfit to undertake the task.

The knowledge he acquired by early reading was erased by his political experience and what he had acquired since was by attrition and of the most unreliable character. He often talked with great energy, but it was like one lost in a wilderness trying by loud shouting to attract attention and succor. He was in constant danger of being entrapped by his adversary and what success he had was attained by main strength and awkwardness.

He was so frequently defeated because of his ignorance of the law and the technical rules of procedure, so often did justice flounder and miscarry because of his inability to guide her, that he lost confidence in the courts, became sour, sarcastic and vituperative against the occupants of the bench, acquired a hatred for the successful and could not favorably consider any question arising in litigation.

At that point the one who might have been a great lawyer became a sad, disappointed and unsuccessful politician. There are many other ways by which the lawyer is lured into politics besides the two we have pointed out. His fellow citizens may induce him to accept office in some branch of the government that he may engraft on the statute some special notion entertained by him or he may resort to political work for notoriety and acquaintance; but through whatever gate he enters if he once gets well into the fray, he will probably never return to the practice of his profession with undivided zeal and consecration.

***

My views on this subject will probably be sharply challenged by the reader. He will recall the names of many famous politicians who were lawyers, and ask if the writer does not consider them well qualified as such? My answer is, if there have been any expert politicians who have in fact been fully equipped lawyers, up to date in all the learning of the profession, who have been fully posted in the latest decisions and acts of legislature, the rules of practice and of evidence, then they are exceptions.

I do not say that such a union is impossible but only that it is not likely to occur. It is very hazardous for the public to employ a politician for legal work, and the fact that they often do so accounts for much of the lack of success which they have in their legal business. Where private parties engage the services of notorious politicians to conduct important suits, they seldom receive the worth of their money.

These notorious men exact excessive pay for their services and in most cases contribute no strength to the case, but stir the opposition into greater efforts, cause the suit to become notorious, put the judge and jury on parade and make the proceeding last a much longer time than it otherwise would. When the public becomes sufficiently discriminating, they will no more think of employing a politician to try a lawsuit than to perform a surgical operation or to design a great public work. The ambitious beginner should decide which profession he prefers and if he decides to be a lawyer concentrate his entire efforts in that direction.

CHAPTER VII.
The Business Agent.

Lawyers are often consulted relative to the conduct of business enterprises. This practice has grown until a large part of the world's business is directed and controlled by persons who originally started out for a professional career. From counsellors in matters of law the transition is easy to advisers in the conduct of business, and from the latter position the path is direct to a point where the lawyer becomes a mere business agent.

By such most of the great estates left in the hands of inexperienced heirs are managed and the great corporations and combinations are formed and directed. The lawyer sometimes inherits or acquires wealth of his own and embarks in such enterprises on his own account. Persons combining a legal training with the ordinary business capacity and appetite for gain are usually more than a match for competitors who have had no such training, and they often acquire great fortunes. But the effect of this departure is serious upon the profession of the law and upon public morals.

The false notion prevails that one who has been once admitted to the bar should be reckoned as a lawyer as long as he lives and all the high crimes, misdemeanors, trickery and fraudulent practices indulged in by these business agents are charged to the legal profession. These vampires of greed are merely prostituting their little knowledge of the law for fraudulent purposes. They are not in any sense real lawyers and their depredations should not be charged to the profession. The lawyer should care more for knowledge and skill in his profession than for wealth.

His clients will cheerfully provide him with all the money he requires in the habits of life fitted to his career. An intelligent management of his affairs will free him from financial entanglements, and he need not seek wealth for wealth's sake. He should have ever before his mind the image of legal justice and his dearest quest should be to ascertain the exact facts and the precise law necessary to obtain it. But all those who practice law do not entertain such exalted ideas. Many have so conducted themselves as to merit the gibe contained in the story told of a highwayman, whose victim remained silent while being deprived of all his clothing but when the Knight of the road began to tear off his porous plaster he inquired where the robber had learned to practice law.

Let me show the genesis of this brand of lawyers.

Handy Skinner

Handy Skinner's father was a horse trader. His mother kept a grocery store. He early exhibited the trading instinct. One of his first questions when he met you was "Have you anything to trade?"

He was always anxious to trade anything or everything which he possessed for something that you possessed, provided of course that he could get the best of the bargain. His small, sharp, brown eyes, thin face, hawk nose, and pointed chin, gave him a shrewd appearance. His motions were catlike. He was always pumping for information and imparting none himself, except such as would be to his personal advantage or aid him in the deal that he was conducting.

It was reported that he had traded an old crippled horse for his license to practice law. If he ever parted with any money it was after he had exhausted every effort to pay in trade. In the practice of the law he exhibited great ingenuity in getting his clients so tangled up with him in the litigation that they could not or dared not discharge him. When he met persons he began at once to inquire into their private affairs and family history to ascertain if they did not have some claims or rights which might be the subject of litigation, and as soon as he could find a pretext he would volunteer advice and urge them to place the matter in his hands.

If it was necessary, he would share in the litigation and even maintain it by paying the cost and expenses. Many persons were thereby made to believe that they had suffered wrongs and when the litigation was well under way, he so managed the matter that they could not get out of the meshes in which he had entangled them.

The first suit was sure to breed others which were themselves only parents of a numerous progeny of other suits. Rare indeed was the instance where a client escaped his clutches until all his means were exhausted.

In the County where Skinner practiced law there were two prosperous farmers, who owned adjoining farms on which they had lived as neighbors in peace and harmony for many years. One day a pig belonging to one rubbed down a board in the partition fence and got into the other's potato patch and rooted open a few hills of half-grown potatoes. The damage was slight and would probably have passed unnoticed had not the owner of the potatoes met Skinner on the street and been made acutely conscious of his loss.

Skinner obtained his consent to bring a suit on shares. In less than ten days the entire neighborhood was thrown into a ferment. The populace divided into parties, nearly an equal number taking sides with each farmer. Slander and vituperation were peddled promiscuously by both sides. Ancient sores were ripped open and made to bleed afresh, and the strife grew hotter and spread wider until finally the case came on for trial. Many witnesses were summoned by each side to impeach the character of those on the opposing side for truth and veracity. The case was on trial for many days during which time the newspapers reprinted the slanders brought out in the testimony and Skinner improved every opportunity for fanning the flames of discord to discover new causes of action.

When this trial was finished the case was appealed. He also brought several slander suits and one libel suit engendered by the bitterness of the potato controversy. He was also employed in four cases of assault and battery, civil and criminal, growing out of the same matter between members of the two families, all of which were appealed, and some were reversed and tried anew. The cost of the various cases including attorneys' fees was so great that the farmer who had started to recover for a few hills of potatoes not only lost his entire crop but had to sell his farm at a great sacrifice to Skinner for money to pay the expenses and attorneys' fees.

But this was not all. Many collateral suits were obtained by the ingenious Skinner. Other neighbors who had been drawn into the maelstrom of the conflict became infuriated toward each other and stimulated by the advice of Skinner discovered that they too had old wrongs that needed redress, so they joined the procession to financial ruin under his guidance.

Nor was this the end. These numerous suits caused a political feud to spring up among the parties and a mismanagement of the County's finances to be alleged, and suits to recover funds that one party charged the other with embezzling. Skinner got the board of Supervisors to employ him in these suits and thus got both arms into the County treasury up to the elbows. He made these suits so expensive that the County had to issue bonds to pay the costs.

These bonds were sold in the east and when time for payment arrived, they were under the advice of Skinner repudiated and the Federal Court was invoked to compel the levy of a tax to pay them. The board under Skinner's advice refused to comply with the writ of mandamus issued by the court and were sent to jail. The litigation then became widespread; some of the cases were taken to the Court of Appeals and then to the Supreme Court of the United States.

The intense excitement and malice thus engendered affected politics in the Congressional District and throughout the

State, and finally when the presidential campaign came on the State being a close one the controversy assumed national importance and determined the election of the president. During the raging of this suit many other suits connected with them sprang up like mushrooms everywhere and wherever a fresh one started Skinner was on hand to sustain and prolong its existence and harvest the fruit.

But he did not rely solely upon fees paid in lawsuits for his profits. These fees were mere incidents; and the suits only introductions to the general business of the clients. Into this business he would pry and onto it he would fasten like a leech, until his connection became secure enough and he had the entire business of the client within his control, then he manipulated it to his own advantage and the client's undoing.

The pig that rubbed down the board filled the township with bankrupts, saddled an enormous debt on the County, changed the politics of a State, elected a president of a nation and became Skinner's steppingstone to affluence.

Skinner rapidly accumulated money and as soon as he got it, he used it to accumulate more patronage. He would buy one share of stock in a corporation to get into a stockholder's meeting, get acquainted with the business, and use his influence to promote litigation. He bought claims against business houses which he thought were short of money and in the name of a stool pigeon forced the institution into bankruptcy or in the hands of a receiver, then gave the proceedings such direction as to sacrifice the property of the insolvent at a forced sale and became himself either directly or indirectly the purchaser. He was especially skillful in the management of the estates of deceased persons to transfer the bulk of the fortune into his own pocket and leave widows and orphans empty handed.

As his riches grew, he collected about him a number of employees suited to affect his purposes. They kept close watch for opportunities to buy into a litigation or to strip those whom misfortune had slain. Like buzzards over a wounded animal he and his agents hovered about the failing debtor eager to profit by his misfortune. Finally, Skinner attracted the attention of the bold pirates of finance who hunt only for big game, and plot to rob the entire population of cities, states, nations, and even empires.

They sought to use him as a tool to affect their nefarious purposes. Beginning as a servant he managed their affairs so adroitly that he soon became their master and ultimately a financial king. At last he arose to such power that even the world's greatest monarchs begged financial assistance and mercy from him.

***

The instinct for trade combined with a corrupt conscience and some knowledge of law created one of the oppressors of mankind.

CHAPTER VIII. Avarice

In the previous CHAPTER on the "business agent" I sought to show how greed may ultimately deflect a lawyer from his profession and make him a despoiler of mankind. I now wish to point out the way it may make him a buccaneer in the profession.

Grabbem and Fleecem

The great firm of Grabbem & Fleecem, did a "land office" business. It kept a press agent, whose duties were to advertise every appearance or connection that the firm had with any important case and to parade the doings of its members before the public.

It had many soliciting agents who examined the newspapers and court dockets and got the first account of all controversies likely to get into court and were early on the spot offering the services of this firm and claiming that it possessed great influence with the judges; that it had peculiar experience and skill for the particular case and were prepared to take it upon terms much cheaper than any others in the profession. Members of this firm gave banquets to judges, procured themselves to be toast masters at these and speakers at trade and club banquets.

They joined prominent churches, were members of the principal fraternities, belonged to all the leading political parties, solicited and procured employment by various officials of the city, state and nation. They became stockholders in all kinds of corporations and established relations with every department of business, official, charitable, and even criminal.

Never for a moment did they show any scruples or relax their efforts to acquire all the legal business they could. Their offices covered an entire floor of a large building wherein they employed clerks at the lowest salaries. Outside they retained policemen, nurses, physicians, real estate agents, superintendents of hospitals and even clergymen, to all of whom they paid a commission on business brought to this firm.

To show the way this firm acquired business I will give one instance. An old Quaker while walking on a cement sidewalk after a shower was made to slip and fall by stepping on a large angle worm. His injuries if any were very slight and the city in no way to blame. But it happened that a solicitor from the firm of Grabbem & Fleecem saw him fall and immediately rushed to his assistance exclaiming: "Oh! You poor man! How terribly you are hurt. What a shame! You must sue the city for this. Go to a hospital immediately." The Quaker protested that he was not injured, but the solicitor called a cab bundled him into it and took him to the hospital.

There he was immediately grabbed by an interne pulled into a private room, stripped of his clothing, put to bed, his ankle bandaged with splints, a surgeon sent for, nurses employed and the Quaker kept under medical treatment for several weeks. The solicitor gave him the card of Grabbem & Fleecem stating that they were the greatest lawyers on earth, could influence courts, control juries, procure witnesses, and get judgments in all cases, and while riding to the hospital he insisted that the Quaker was seriously injured both internally and externally and that the best treatment was necessary to save his life.

His nurses at the hospital commented constantly upon his miserable appearance and on the terrible wrong which he had suffered and the necessity of his employing the firm of Grabbem & Fleecem. The interne physicians sang the same song on every occasion. The surgeon who called to see him looked very solemn, spoke of his injuries in sepulchral tones and expressed grave doubts of a complete recovery. He also urged the Quaker to secure the services of this firm to collect damages from the city.

Many of the Quaker's friends male and female called, looked upon him with pitying glances, magnified his injuries and insisted that he take immediate action against the city and employ this great firm. But the Quaker remained obdurate. His conscience was opposed to litigation.

Finally his pastor called and made a long prayer over him in which he inserted good words for Grabbem & Fleecem. The Quaker wavered but he did not yield. The medicines given him internally, the liniments that had been rubbed on, the opiates injected to allay his imaginary pain and induce sleep, the statements of his nurses and physicians, combined with the doleful prognostications of his friends and the prayers of his pastor must have convinced him that he had received some injury, but he would have held out to the last but for a frightful dream. He dreamed that his injuries had caused his death and that his soul was wafted to the Celestial city, that when he applied at the gate for admission.

Saint Peter presented him the card of Grabbem & Fleecem announcing that they were the greatest lawyers in heaven and the only ones permitted to plead before the judgment seat, that their offices occupied the entire sky-parlor at the

Saint's Rest, and that Peter urged him to engage this great firm to present his cause before the great white throne. The Quaker was greatly distressed at this for he was still opposed to employing lawyers. So, he sat down on a cloud and meditated. At last he concluded to go to the other place.

There he was ushered into the brimstone room where he was presented to a solemn looking sprite whose long dark garments partially concealed a cloven hoof. This sprite handed him a card which glowed in letters of fire: "Satan, Senior Partner of Grabbem & Fleecem" owns courts, manufactures evidence, suborns witnesses, deals in verdicts and sells judgments and decrees to the highest bidder. His offices occupy the whole basement in the infernal regions." Thereupon the Quaker raised his hands in horror and exclaimed: "Surely this is Hell!" and awoke.

The dream so preyed upon him that he was finally induced to yield to the solicitations of the firm and engage them. In a few days a receipt was presented to him to sign acknowledging that the city had paid him three thousand dollars for injuries consisting of a ruptured ligament, a floating kidney, and a concussion of the spine. At the same time the firm presented a statement of their account which showed that after deducting commissions paid to solicitors, nurses, doctors, ministers, hospital expenses, and fees for his and the city's attorney there was coming to the Quaker for his share the sum of $43.

Sometimes this firm settled with a client for a moderate fee stipulating they would be permitted to advertise the receipt of compensation amounting to hundreds of thousands of dollars. They kept many trumpets blowing the assertion that they were the world's greatest lawyers. They became rich not only out of the fools that are said to be born every minute but from the patronage of some level-headed men.

***

Many persons showing great sagacity in other departments of life who can manage general business with consummate skill are caught by the glaring advertisements of such firms as Grabbem & Fleecem and are induced to trust their lives and fortunes in such hands. They cheerfully pay exorbitant prices for the miserable service received, when there are hundreds of good honest lawyers of much greater skill and learning who have plenty of time to attend to their cases at a fraction of the price paid to such shysters.

A moment's thought would seem to be sufficient for an intelligent person to see that lawyers like Grabbem & Fleecem are not likely to bestow careful attention upon matters left in their hands; that the money spent by them in commissions and advertising must necessarily come out of the dupes thus snared into their offices, and the energy expended in conducting such a machine must be taken from the stock required to conduct cases.

The lawyer should take no more business than he has time and ability to manage well. If he exerts himself to control a much greater quantity all his tasks are imperfectly done, and those who patronize him are made to suffer from his inability to give their matters proper attention or from the incompetency and infidelity of the employees to whom he has entrusted their affairs. Some persons are capable of doing more work in the same time than others equally learned, but it is the opinion of the writer that an important case containing a sharp controversy relative to law and evidence will ordinarily require at least two weeks to prepare and try it. Many such controversies require more than a month.

A good lawyer ought not to attempt more than twenty-five a year. On account of the large amount of other work which ordinarily comes to a trial lawyer twelve important cases a year is likely to be the full limit of his capacity, provided they are closely contested. Yet so greedy are such men as Grabbem & Fleecem that they will engage themselves to handle hundreds of cases yearly and then delay and thus discommode their clients or imperil their interests by putting the management of the suits in the hands of incompetent clerks.

Avarice has a blasting effect upon all professions. The surgeon whose mind is on the pocket book of the helpless patient, the preacher whose prayers are intended for the purses of his flock, the editor whose pen is guided by the magnetism of money, these are bad enough, but the lawyer whose mind is bent on money getting to the exclusion of all other considerations is worse. He is wholly unfit for use in the administration of justice.

The lawyer's heart should be in his work. He should consider his profession as noble and worthy of his best efforts. He should love it and find in it his chief delight. That his judgment may be unclouded it is better that he feels no peculiar interest in the success or failure of the litigation. If a lawyer has the proper love for his profession he will not care to join in the chase for wealth, fame, or public office. He will leave these for men with lowlier ideals, for they are all greatly inferior to the services he renders in the attainment of justice.

It is essential that he have this appreciation and love for his profession in order that he may consecrate himself to it, enjoy it and render to humanity the important service which it must obtain from the members of the bar. Those who aspire to great wealth or political glory may have been educated for the bar, but when they have decided to worship at another shrine they ought not to hold themselves out as lawyers. The relation of attorney and client is of such a delicate nature that it should not be complicated with any other business affairs.

The lawyer in his dealing with his client should confine himself strictly to the scope of his profession, rendering only professional services. He should not be a borrower from his client or a lender to him, nor should he become interested with his client in any investment or become entangled socially or politically with him. Whenever the lawyer steps out of the strictly professional relation he starts a train of thought and worry which deprives him of his composure and the time necessary to keep posted on his profession. He also becomes exposed to temptation and the subject of suspicion likely to imperil his standing in the estimation of his client.

The standard here raised may be considered too high to be practicable but the nearer the lawyer can approach it, the greater will be the skill and knowledge which he will acquire and the larger the degree of satisfaction and pleasure which will come to him from the pursuit of his profession.

CHAPTER IX. Disorder

Order is essential everywhere from the government of a country to the management of a prize fight. Disorder causes friction, confusion, delay and defeat. The lawyer has to deal with complicated matters of great importance and must act quickly at the time appointed. Necessity for system in his affairs can hardly be over-stated. When his case is reached, he must be ready with the authorities that sustain his view of the law and with the documents and witnesses that prove his contention as to the facts. These constitute the chain upon which his hopes depend and if one link be missing, he will meet with disaster. He should have all where he can produce it quickly, or he must ask for delay, become confused and see the court irritated by the loss of time thus caused or have his case disposed of on a record less favorable than it should be.

The lawyer's fees are always considered high by those required to pay them and the lawyer who lays upon his client a burden out of proportion to the result accomplished will incur his displeasure and make him disgusted with legal proceedings. To secure ample compensation for the time used the lawyer must accomplish the result aimed at in as short time as possible. To reach the minimum in this particular it is necessary that his work be so systematized as to exclude waste and useless repetitions. He should do everything for a purpose and if possible, finish it while at it.

He should keep a record of his doings, copies of every paper, statements from every witness and have all where it can be quickly found, so that the case when once prepared for trial is prepared for all time, save for such additions as newly discovered evidence and recently reported cases may require. The time thus consumed should be accurately charged when expended. If the result of the case makes it necessary to reduce the charges credit can be given, or if it will allow an increase it is an easy matter to add thereto.

The lawyer should have an office provided with the best appliances, supplied with all the latest publications and equipped with trained and experienced clerks. This office should be so managed that everything will have a place where it will be kept in perfect order. First of all, the lawyer must be in his place, and on time and personally observe the rules of order which he has laid down. Many are the lawyers who work without system and great are the losses sustained by them and their clients on account thereof. Here is an illustration.

Captain Jehosaphat Jehu

Captain Jehosaphat Jehu, was a very active man. Like a cyclone loaded with sticks, stones and all kinds of dirt he moved creating excitement, wonder and confusion wherever he appeared. He observed no principles of order. He acted upon impulse, and a powerful impulse it was. What education he had he had obtained in an irregular manner and the subjects which he considered were determined by accident. Some of his knowledge had been caught on the fly, some had been thrown at him and a considerable portion had been kicked into him.

If he ran onto a book, he began to read it and continued until something else pushed him away. If in conversation he encountered a person sufficiently pugnacious and aggressive to edge in a word, Jehu might get an idea. When severely licked in a suit or otherwise jolted by disappointment his mind was provided with an impression which clung to him for a considerable time.

Anyway, he had no system either of collecting or retaining knowledge and most of his notions were evolved from his inner consciousness. The few which he had effervesced with such force that he could crow down his opponents in any discussion depending upon lungs for its termination. He was tall, thin, long jointed, and bony. His clothes were misfits, and usually looked like the garments of a scarecrow. His hair was generally unkempt, his ponderous moustache, and scraggy beard badly soiled. His clothing was usually stained with a large variety of substances. If he lacked buttons to hold his garments in place a nail, a safety-pin, or any kind of string were made to do duty and while he had one suspender, he was ready for action.

He had a den which he called an office. To this his mail was sent, and he appeared there at irregular intervals, but none could foretell when his next appearance would be or how long he might remain. In this place he had an old table, a dilapidated bookcase and some broken sets of books. Some of the books were in the case, others on the table, or on the floor, but wherever they were they were well covered with dust, which did not matter, for he so seldom used them.

His table was littered with an irregular bunch of legal papers, memoranda, newspapers, old books, letters and such other things a happened to be thrown there. All were tangled in a confused mass, so that whatever found its way to this table was likely to be lost when wanted.

There were many loafers sitting in the old chairs adding to them from time to time a fresh veneer of greasy substance and digging a few more dents in the already badly mutilated furniture. They passed the time in playing cards, talking politics or religion, distributing everyday gossip or telling smutty stories, or boasting of their conquests in love or law. To this den Jehu would come with a rush, fumble around among the papers on his table, talk a few moments with some of the denizens, tell a yarn or two, then rush off to some appointment or to court, and in the course of time return again and repeat the operation.

He was rarely on time and often had his cases dismissed or continued because he was late. When a case came on for trial, he was usually without some of his witnesses and always without books to prove his assertions and was generally in a helpless confusion on account of his lack of systematic preparation.

The judge might be well disposed toward his client and desire to try his case upon its merits, but he was handicapped by the failure of Jehu to provide the basis for a favorable decision. So, notwithstanding his intense activity and the rush and rattle that accompanied all his motions, Jehu usually suffered defeat.

To make clear to the general reader how the lack of orderly preparation brought Jehu and his clients to grief, I will give a few of his mistakes.

After several days spent in trying a suit for damages against a Street R. R. Co., a verdict was ordered against him because he had failed to prove that the company operating the road was the one sued. He was engaged to prosecute a man for a crime and the defendant was acquitted because he failed to prove that the place where the crime was committed was in the county where the indictment was found.

He brought suit for a divorce, took a great amount of evidence but failed because he did not prove that the complainant had been a resident of the state long enough to give the court jurisdiction.

He was defeated in one action on a fire insurance policy, after several days' trial because he did not show that proofs of loss were made to the company or waived by it, and defeated in another because the suit was brought before the claim was due under the policy.

Many times he lost because his evidence did not agree with the allegations in his pleadings. His appeals to the Upper Courts were frequently rendered useless on account of his failing to take proper exceptions to the action of the court below. Such appeals were often dismissed because not taken in time or because taken to the wrong court.

***

None but those who have had experience can realize the sharp agony that pierces a lawyer's heart when he learns that his defeat is due to his own folly. When he looks upon the ghastly face of his disappointed client and thinks of the victory he might have won, he curses himself and groans inwardly and searches his distracted mind for an excuse to mitigate his blunder.

He hears the chuckling of his triumphant adversary, the jeers and prophesies of his enemies, the vain commiseration of his pitying friends. He feels that he is the foolish fish that jumped at a fly and caught a hook; that he is the silly rabbit that ran into the trap, that he is the wild gosling caught in the subtle fowler's snare. The general who has led his army into an ambush and had it cut to pieces, as he gazes on the scattered remnants of his once proud host feels all the anguish of the damned.

But his distress is no greater than that of the conscientious lawyer who realizes that his own folly has ruined his trusting client. But men like Jehu endure many such experiences. It seems strange they do not discover that their sad defeats come from a lack of orderly preparation and thus be led to change their habits. But they never do. They become calloused and continue the blunders from year to year making more and greater mistakes as they grow older until death puts an end to their depredations. So, it was with Jehu.

So many of his cases ended disastrously that he could not accumulate more than a mere subsistence, was always in debt and kept in hot water during his entire professional career. He attracted many clients, but they were very poor people, who were as ignorant as they were poor and they wasted his time and he wasted theirs.

There is no prescription more potent to prevent mistakes than the adoption and strict observance of wise rules of order. By this method a man of ordinary gifts can render a great service at the bar; without it the brightest minds become the playthings of chance, and suffer the most disastrous defeats where they should have won brilliant victories.

Surely the poet was not far wrong when he wrote "Order is heaven's first law."

CHAPTER X. Cowardice

A lawyer should not be a coward for he must often lead in the fiercest intellectual combats. The leaders of armies have plenty of company. The leaders of political movements have throngs of backers. The lawyer must stand alone in many of the fights which he makes for the property, liberty or life of his clients. Those interested in his success are usually helpless and furnish him no intellectual or moral support. They are ignorant of the law.

They are unfamiliar with the rules of proceeding and they must be silent spectators while he conducts alone the intellectual warfare in their behalf. Thus, he needs the rarest quality of courage: an ability to hold firmly to his individual opinion against all opposition and to fight for it unwaveringly until every tribunal provided for by the law has been appealed to in vain.

This may not seem so difficult to the inexperienced as it really is. Most of the mankind cannot withstand a strong intellectual opposition. Some may make a great show of courage in the first attack. A small number may suffer one defeat and not waver in either zeal or conviction, but comparatively few are those who can endure repeated defeats, hear the sneering remarks of their opponents, the discouraging counsels of their friends and the groans of their clients at the expense they are incurring and yet experience no flagging in zeal or diminution in the firmness of purpose.

Fewer still are those rare spirits who can receive the buffetings of evil fortune wholly undisturbed, who can smile at adversity and all its vexatious accompaniments, and with a serene soul proceed as regularly in the discharge of duty as a nicely adjusted clock ticks out the time, though multitudes perish and dynasties rise and fall. A soul thus fortified is adapted to endure the vexations of the trial lawyer. In such hands the greatest cause is likely to receive the best attention.

Unfortunately many members of the bar are devoid of this courage. They do not sufficiently prepare their cases to lay the basis of a well-grounded conviction. They approach the contest with fear and trembling and at the first unfavorable intimation from the court they are unnerved. By a disastrous defeat they are panic stricken. During a heated trial the fear of losing induces such a tremor that they lose sleep, turn and toss all night upon their restless beds racking their brains with worry, and if the trial is protracted over many days they become seriously disabled before the end is reached.

This causes them to omit many things that ought to be done and to say and do many things in their bewilderment that ought not to be said or done. They cannot contemplate defeat without pain or converse with their disappointed client without giving fictitious excuses for it. This causes the client to lose his courage and he decides to submit to injustice rather than incur the risk of another trial, or if he musters nerve enough to appeal the attorney so shattered by defeat is unfit to enter another struggle.

The morally brave man makes no parade of his courage. He does not even think of it for he always has it with him in good working order. The coward who ever feels the lack of it tries to cover the defect by assuming a brave demeanor. He blows, storms, threatens, and protests that he is not afraid. He repeatedly declares that nothing can bend or turn him. He struts, swaggers, swears and assumes the prowess of the "god of war."

The brave man does none of these but coolly gathers his strength, watches his opportunity and strikes. What he has to do he does timely, directly, and effectively, and not with exhaustion, but out of the fullness of his strength. Having struck once he stands firm ready to strike again as often as occasion requires. The man who has true moral courage is never without it. Disappointment, defeat, and even death does not dismay. Awakened suddenly from a sound sleep his nerves are firm and ready for action. Struck from ambush unexpectedly, he squares himself calmly for the fray.

Friends desert him, foes multiply, but he wavers not. He has within a spark of that divine power which stands eternally strong amid the wreck of worlds. As a spurious imitation of a brave man I take the risk of introducing

General Bluff

From youth he pretended to be a fighter. He was always bullying his schoolmates, and playmates. He carried a chip on his shoulder and dared anyone to knock it off. He took special delight in imposing on those younger and weaker than himself. He was very offensive in his treatment of the opposite sex. He annoyed all persons by boasting of his conquests and terrorized many of the timid by his noisy and threatening oaths.

When he grew to manhood, he was undersized and not especially strong physically, but he had a head like a bulldog, small cruel black eyes, bushy eyebrows, an immense moustache which he waxed with an upward turn at the sides, a bald head, fringed with a few coarse hairs, a snub nose, a mouth like a slit in an oak board, and lips as destitute of expression as an Egyptian hieroglyphic. When he screwed his countenance into a threatening aspect it reminded one of a pumpkin jack lantern. He was not familiar with law or legal proceedings except that portion employed in collecting debts. He experienced great glee in grinding a distressed debtor.

He swelled with magnificent pride as he strutted into the hovel of poverty and threatened to turn its wretched inmates into the street, unless they paid a bill he had to collect. His soul was in an ecstasy when he got an opportunity of writing an insulting letter to some timid girl promising her all kinds of vexatious persecution if she did not call at his office and settle the account he held. With fiendish delight he would wing the last penny from the withered hands of want and apply it on his illegal and extortionate fees. Yet he was usually careful not to come within reach of people who were able to defend themselves and were disposed to do so.

Once he called a sleepy looking country boy a liar. The rustic invited him out into the road, and with great pretensions of courage he went. He danced around the slow-motioned son of the soil, like a king bird around a hawk, sawing the air with his clenched fists and exclaiming: "I'll lick you to death, you greenhorn ! " all of which he emphasized with ear piercing oaths.

The quiet stripling watched his maneuvers until he came near enough then gave Bluff a left hander over the eye that felled him like a dead fish. He was dragged to a hotel nearby and soaked with water until he came to consciousness. His left eye was swollen shut and looked like a piece of raw beef. He claimed the countryman struck him with brass knuckles but of course that was not true.

Ever afterward Bluff prudently avoided close contact with persons who might be capable of protecting themselves and he exhibited his bravado while under the protection of a judge or other officers of the law or when in the presence of frightened women and children or with members of the legal profession who were not likely to resort to physical force.

Amid such surroundings he bellowed like the "bull of Bashan, " he showed his big front teeth like a hyena among the tombs, he pushed out his chest like a Roman Gladiator, he stood like Ajax defying the lightning, and swore oaths that would shame a drunken sailor.

These vulgar trappings caught the eye of many foolish clients and he gained credit for being a stubborn fighter. Many employed him to attend to their cases, because, they believed him to be strong and courageous. But he was at heart the basest of cowards. What was accounted courage was only cruelty.

When he met his match, his veins were full of skimmed milk. His spine shook like a lamb's tail, and he sought the first excuse to fly. He had neither nerve enough to stand and fight nor courage enough to admit that he was mistaken. He always sought to lay the blame for disaster on someone else and then would crawl into his hole and stay there until he got another opportunity to brag and threaten.

It is sometimes said that the brave know no fear. This is false. All but imbeciles feel fear. The coward feels it, quakes and flies. The brave man feels it but stands and fights. The first places his personal safety above his duty, the last puts his duty above his personal safety. Cowardice is therefore another name for selfishness. Hence the brave man is courteous and kind to the weak and just even to his enemies. The coward tramples down and crushes the helpless to exalt himself and plunders all that he can with impunity.

In order that he may love justice and fight to obtain and sustain it against all the forces that fraud can raise against it, the lawyer should of all men be mentally, morally and spiritually brave, and he must be so to attain the highest excellence in his profession.

CHAPTER XI.
Confidence in the Court

Most lawyers are sometimes and many lawyers are many times disabled in their advocacy of a cause by a lack of confidence in the integrity and intelligence of the Judge. No one can as efficiently conduct a trial when he thinks his evidence and arguments will be disregarded. The thought paralyzes his brain, takes away his zeal and tends to make him irritable to a high degree. He becomes discourteous to the court, makes the Judge feel his lack of confidence and he too is thus prevented from giving the case a fair and unbiased attention.

That lawyer is best equipped for his task who has faith in the intelligence and integrity of the occupant of the bench which nothing can shake. Questions of law may be decided against him. His confidence continues. Erroneous expressions relative to his evidence may be made. He suspects no wrong. The Court may even reverse itself to give the victory to his adversary, and yet amid the stings of defeat he never doubts the honesty and competency of the occupant of the Bench.

The lawyer who has this faith must add to a generous nature the charity which comes from a wide experience and a clear knowledge of human frailty in matters of opinion. How few possess these qualities.

It has long been customary for the ablest lawyers to impugn the intelligence and integrity of the Judge who has decided against them. From the courtroom where they have met with disaster they have retired to the tavern, the saloon, or the street corner and have given vent to their feelings by inveighing furiously against the Judge and jury. Frequently during the progress of the trial, they have lost their tempers and become very bitter in their resentment because the Judge has failed to agree with them upon propositions of law or evidence.

So narrow minded have they been in their zeal that they could conceive no room for an honest difference of opinion. The mere fact that their arguments have not been effective has been considered conclusive proof that the Judge is incompetent or corrupt. Thus, they have tried to browbeat the

Judge and intimidate him into finding in their favor to avoid encountering their displeasure.

Judges are but lawyers on the bench and often lawyers with but little experience. The more anxious they are to do right the more sensitive they become to such manifestations. It is difficult under such circumstances for them to retain that composure and concentration of mind essential to the forming of a correct judgment. Where the Judge is not intimidated by such conduct he may become unconsciously prejudiced against his assailant and thus be prevented from giving him so fair a hearing as the law contemplates. Some persons are by nature suspicious and believe that all men have a price, and that most are fools.

Thomas Doubt

Thomas Doubt was that kind. He looked upon human society as corrupt in all its strata. He considered the general government of his country a criminal conspiracy organized for plunder, and the world generally as the personal property of Satan, created for damnation. His eyes were so focused that he saw nothing but defects.

A bright day was a weather breeder. Flush times the precursors of the coming panic. A friendly smile a false pretense. A generous gift a device to get an underhold. There was no such thing as love. There was nothing like honor. Every person was a liar and the best ought to be in the penitentiary. Every breeze, though sweet with perfume swarmed Avid microbes of a malignant character. Every flower was a shield that covered a serpent. He was always running the gauntlet between files of enemies who were plotting to destroy him. From earliest infancy he had always been cheated and deceived.

He regarded his birth as a calamity. He found no comfort in the society of his family or friends. The common amusements of people were looked upon by him with disgust and pronounced the frivolity of fools. The press was subsidized. The pulpit filled with hired liars. Commerce was obtaining money under false pretenses. All kinds of business were dishonest or criminal in their character. He wished to extract the honey of this life from the gall of his enemies.

He adopted the law as a profession to punish them. He saw no beauty in its doctrine, he took no pride in its traditions. The honored names of its founders evoked no enthusiasm. Relative to some he had collected evidence to prove that they were scoundrels and those against whom he had no evidence he assumed were like the others. Of the occupants of the bench, he considered those in the highest seats the worst criminals and the greatest enemies of mankind. His scent for faults was so largely developed that he not only exaggerated all defects which he could find, but imagined many that did not exist. At the same time, he was deaf and blind to all evidence showing the existence of truth, beauty, honor, justice and love in the world.

How could such a man learned though he was in all the lore of his profession, industrious as he was in collecting and amassing his evidence, faithful as he was in zeal and fidelity to his clients, yet so saturated with distrust, be able to effectively discharge his duty as a trial lawyer? He carried into court an atmosphere charged with wormwood. He fell out with the Judge and became unpopular with the jury. He was despised by the opposing party, incurred the lasting enmity of his lawyer and frequently lost the confidence of his own client and had to sue to get his fees.

Yet such were his talents that he received a large patronage and became one of the greatest railroad lawyers in his state in the defense of suits for personal injuries.

In his youth he had learned the trade of a blacksmith and got his rudimentary education while working at the forge. He was a physical giant and he tried his lawsuits with hammers and tongs and great and steady were the blows he sometimes struck. I will illustrate his manner of treating the court by one incident.

He had brought a suit for a lady against a saloonkeeper for selling beer to her husband. The state law made it a crime to sell beer to a person in the habit of becoming intoxicated. He put a witness on the stand and asked him if he had ever seen the husband drunk? The opposing lawyer objected and the Judge without hearing any argument sustained the objection. Mr. Doubt then looked at the Judge with a surprised expression on his face and repeated the question. "Objection sustained, " exclaimed the Judge with some irritation. He then arose, adjusted his eyeglasses and stared at the Judge and asked with a voice trembling with emotion, yet severely sarcastic: "Is it possible that you hold that I can't show that this woman's husband was in the habit of becoming intoxicated?"

"I have sustained the objection, " retorted the Judge with emphasis.

Mr. Doubt then grabbed the statute convulsively, opened it and held it in his left hand, and gesticulating furiously with his right spoke in tones so loud as to be heard in every part of the room. Every word was uttered so slowly and forcibly that it fell like a sledge on the Judge's ears: "Law provides that it is a crime to sell beer to a person in the habit of becoming intoxicated. I propose to show that this scoundrel (pointing to the blear-eyed bloated defendant) sold beer to this poor woman's husband (pointing to the plaintiff, a delicate lady with large sorrowful eyes), until he dragged him going down into the very gutter. And there you sit and say I can't show it! My God! is this a court of justice!" As he uttered these last words the very air was vibrant with wrath, not only that of the speaker but with the indignation of the crowd of onlookers who now saw the court's error.

It was too sultry for the Judge. The hot blush of shame came to his temples as he said: "Mr. Doubt, if that is what you want it for you may show it." Instead of letting the discomfited Judge down easy Doubt insisted upon twisting the hook in the gills of the fish he had landed. He screwed his features into an expression of sneering contempt and said in tones that grated viciously; "In heaven's name what did you think I wanted it for?"

"Mr. Doubt, I fine you $25 for contempt," said the Judge angrily.

"Make it fifty, make it a hundred," shouted Doubt. "Twenty-five doesn't begin to express the contempt I feel."

The Judge then raised it to one hundred and Doubt handed his check to the clerk saying; "I am willing to pay for my luxuries. " Of course, when the Judge cooled down, the fine was remitted, and the check returned.

After Doubt had delivered a terrible tirade against the opposite party and the court had adjourned, the party accosted Doubt and asked if what he had said was lawyer's talk or facts. "What's the difference," asked the lawyer. "Why," said he, "if it is lawyer's talk it's all right, but if it's facts I propose to thresh the ground with you."

"What are you talking about, you insignificant, imbecile, papsucker," exclaimed Doubt, "you know if you should meet me on the street you would run like a scared rabbit. If you don't look out, you'll fall in a fit where you stand, you are such a contemptible coward! " Doubt's assailant wilted and slunk away.

He indulged in the pleasures of calumny at the expense of every individual that he knew, and he went still further. He sometimes made an entire class the object of his vituperation. On one occasion he put on the pillory an organization containing 80,000 members.

Among other things he said of them:

"There may be men in other callings who for some single vice would compare with them, but for a combination in harmonious blending of cowardice, deceit, dishonesty, impudence, lechery, and leprous rascality, they stand unrivaled and without a peer." This malicious assault caused the society to demand of the railroad company that employed him that he be discharged and to enforce that demand a general boycott was declared against the road. Its business shrank enormously, and the president called on Doubt for an apology, but his answer was:

"If apologies were as plentiful as blackberries, in the language of Falstaff, I would not give one under compulsion.' " And he did not and was not discharged although his lampoon cost his client an immense sum of money.

While the fever of excitement was at the highest Doubt took the train to go to Court. He was then on crutches and two men seated in front of him were heard by him to remark, that they would like to catch the lawyer who had so defamed them. Doubt astonished them by this interruption:

"I am the man, what do you want? " They looked at each other, and then into his flaming eyes and changed to the next coach. The foregoing instances are a few of the many hundreds that could be told of this peculiar character, who was a great student, a powerful orator, an intrepid fighter and would have taken his place at the head of his profession in the nation, had he not looked with such suspicion and distrust upon his associates.

True he was sometimes correct in his suspicions but oftener wrong than right and always excessive in the quantity of blame and corruption which he supposed others to possess. Yet he had about him a sort of magnetism by which he was able to draw and retain the friendship of many whom he mistreated, and his powerful will forced others to aid him. He became a towering figure in his locality but was compelled to see men greatly inferior to him in learning and natural gifts placed above him and crowned with the laurels of a success which he never could attain because of his lack of confidence in his fellows.

***

Confidence is a kind of cement which holds together the molecules of human society. The lack of it disintegrates and nullifies the best efforts of our race. In the financial world it spells ruin. In the moral world it means dissension, and hatred. But nowhere is the need of confidence greater than in the administration of justice and the place of its greatest need here is in the mind of the lawyer when he presents the cause of his client to the consideration of the court.

CHAPTER XII. Pride

ALL wish to be admired and to do something that will win and deserve admiration. So strong is the passion that multitudes endure distress without complaint, cowards become heroes and misers are made generous. A reasonable degree of pride stimulates the lawyer to excel in his profession and prevents him from sinking into mean and sordid practices.

But pride is often developed to excess and then it becomes a stiff and unnatural dignity, an ever-present consciousness of self; a disposition to subject the interest of the client to the passion of the lawyer for adulation. It then cripples him in the discharge of his duty. I take the case of

Paul Proud

He was a very neat little gentleman who had the best education that wealth could procure. His small round head scantily covered with fine black hair contained more legal maxims than could be found anywhere else in the same space. He probably knew more Roman law than Cicero, more Greek law than Solon, more English law than Edmund Burke and could speak fluently in more languages than all of them put together. And he was an orator after the classic models.

It was a great joy to hear the large words of Greek and Latin derivation emerge from his little mouth and see him strain his symmetrical lips to produce on opening large enough for the passage of their ponderous bulk.

The travail thus experienced in giving birth to his prodigious sentences was assisted somewhat by a vigorous shaking of his head and the tossing of his mane which at times inspired wonder if not terror to his auditors. He could repeat many of the greatest ancient and modern orations, exhibit all the good points and suggest improvements that even Quintilian never thought of. Nor did his capacity end in framing words.

He had the genuine poetic fire, the divine afflatus, which thrills and captures the hearts of multitudes. But he had acquired with these excellences an overweening pride and a wish to be in the center of every stage where the spotlight was the brightest; and to be smothered with the blossoms of unlimited adulation. He could not endure blame nor ridicule, nor was he willing to undertake an unpopular case, or one where he was likely to be identified with a disreputable person.

He was a kid gloved, silk stockinged, sunshine lawyer, and he moved with a grace that was charming and conducted himself with a dignity that seemed majestic to some and ridiculous to others. To show how this great scholar, orator and dignified gentleman was blown from his moorings by a lawyer of much less dignity I must give a short account of a jury trial.

A country merchant in failing circumstances gave several mortgages. The first was to a wholesale firm, the second to his sister for borrowed money, and the third to Proud's client, another wholesale dealer of great wealth. Proud's client declined to accept the third mortgage and treating the others as fraudulent sued out an attachment in the Federal Court and had the United States marshal sell the entire stock. The sister sued the marshal as an ordinary scalawag for trespass, and Proud was engaged by the merchant to defend him.

In order that he might be allowed to make the opening and closing speeches, Proud admitted all the allegations of the girl's claim, but set up the special defense that her mortgage was given to defraud creditors. This entitled the little man to make the last speech. In his first address to the jury he said but a few words, expecting the plaintiff's attorney to make a weak or indifferent answer, and then Proud intended to launch forth in reply a great oration on the despicable character of fraud and thus stampede the jury in favor of his client. But in this he was mistaken, for the plaintiff's attorney knew Proud and determined to take advantage of his weakness and this is the way he proceeded in his address to the jury.

"You have observed, gentlemen, with what anxiety my little friend has striven for the last speech. You may not know why, but I will tell you. He proposes to make the greatest effort of his life! I was present gentlemen, at our new Opera House when he dedicated that palatial temple to the god Momus, and I saw the elite and learned of our city lean forward with craned necks and strained ears as they drank in the honey of his words.

I was present in the Senate during the impeachment proceedings when he pleaded the cause of the one-armed soldier against the nefarious combination that was seeking to despoil him of his honor and his office and I saw the great Senate chloroformed by his majestic periods in behalf of liberty and justice. I was one of that vast multitude who stood with uncovered heads at the east front of the Capitol to hear his eulogy of the world's greatest soldier, the matchless hero of Appomattox, and I saw acres of my fellow countrymen in tears as he told how the angel of death guided the pen of the old hero while he finished his immortal memoirs.

On all these occasions, gentlemen, he was a star of the first magnitude, yea, a veritable sun whose brilliancy made all other orbs look pale. But these efforts, gentlemen, were only small samples of his capacity and today he proposes to surpass them all; he intends to show how eloquent he can be when he is attempting to steal three hundred dollars from a servant girl and give them to a multimillionaire!"

At this point the eyes of the proud little man snapped with anger, and he protested to the court that the speaker was treating him unfairly. The judge laughed and refused to interfere, so the speaker continued:

"Had his client come tome instead of going to my eloquent friend, I would have told him that I considered his case hopeless. I would have said, if you could transfer the action to the mines of Siberia where they hitch their women to coal cars to drag coal out of the mines, or to Tartary where they drown their female infants, or to some Cannibal Island of the sea where they eat women every morning for breakfast, you might bribe a jury to give you a verdict.

But in an Anglo-Saxon country, where we respect and protect our women, — in the United States where the rights of the poorest girl are as sacred as our flag — to expect such a verdict

[103]

from a jury would be the limit of imbecility. But," continued the speaker, "I am no orator like my friend. I have no gift to make juries crazy. He relies on his irresistible powers. But in this, gentlemen, he may be mistaken, for my friend has a kind heart in his diminutive breast and when he thinks of my poor client on her knees in a kitchen, and of the long years she has toiled and waited for justice in this court and that his splendid periods are being prostituted to deprive her of her rights and to enrich an already over-fed and purse bloated millionaire, the thought will palsy his slick tongue, his heart will arise and choke his utterances and his polished dactyls will not flow."

Again, the speaker was interrupted by the little gentleman who was now becoming furious in his rage, so much so that he could scarcely make his objection understood by the court. It was however promptly overruled, and the speaker thus proceeded:

"My atomic opponent is not pleased at my remarks, gentlemen. I am sorry that I have no talent to entertain you as he has, but do not allow my awkwardness to prejudice you against my poor client. Orators, gentlemen, sometimes have poor tastes in the selection of the objects of their eloquence. I am not a warmhearted man like my friend. I have a weather eye for the main chance and often need money, but if I needed it as the drowning man needs air, I could not filch it from this poor girl.

[104]

I would rather be a city scavenger, and clean vaults at midnight ; I had rather follow the wake of an army and pick the pockets of the slain ; I had rather go among the tombs and steal the reeking shanks of dead men from their shrouds and peddle them to doctors' colleges to get pence or porridge to sustain my miserable carcass than to prostitute what talents a merciful God has given me for the purpose of cheating her out of her hard earned money. But not so with this warm-hearted master of magnificent rhetoric. Even now he is sucking wind nigh to bursting preparing to turn himself wrong side out while strutting as a pigeon for the would-be despoiler of this helpless girl."

Again, Proud appealed to the court's protection and was again refused. His color was now ashen, his lips quivered, and he bit them compulsively in his overpowering rage. His opponent continued for half an hour longer in the same manner, and finally closed with these words:

"You have heard me, gentlemen. What I have said is merely an introduction to his great speech. I am a sort of John the Baptist as it were, in advance of the coming king. Whether he will uncap a volcano or break an egg is beyond my knowledge. But I introduce him to you expecting him to deliver the greatest 'spread-eagle speech' of his life." Mr. Proud then arose and spoke about five minutes, calling his opponent a demagogue, a fool, a blatherskite, and stated that the case on trial was not such as justified him in attempting any display of his powers. He then closed and left the court room hurriedly.

The jury retired and, in a few moments, returned a verdict against him. Proud was sent for but refused to return to hear the verdict. When the other case came on for trial, he let it go by default. A thoroughly equipped lawyer should be too thick-skinned to allow ridicule of any kind to irritate him. He should forget himself completely in advocating the cause of his client.

The justice of that cause should fill his -mind with light to, the exclusion of all side lights. He will then be secure against all the arts the opposing counsel may employ to confuse or disable him: If on the contrary the trial lawyer thinks mainly of himself and his own popularity and the credit which he is winning for himself, his senses are liable to be lost in the fog which may be raised by the breath of the opposing counsel.

CHAPTER XIII. Honesty

THE charge of dishonesty has been so frequently made against lawyers that it may be almost considered a proverb, and yet, it is certain that no other class of men is so implicitly trusted without bonds or security; and none has a greater opportunity to profit by corruption and escape discovery. Nor is there anywhere a greater temptation to use trickery and deception for success than in the practice of the law.

Considering the number of persons who practice dishonesty for personal profit in other vocations it would be a wonder if the legal profession were not tainted.

This subject is large enough for a volume, but we must confine our comments to an ordinary chapter and notice a few of the common faults of lawyers in this respect hoping to accomplish a lasting good to the profession.

First: The lawyer should certainly be honest with his client at all times and under all circumstances.

He should not assure his client of success or even give his opinion that success is probable until he has exhausted all available sources of knowledge on which he should base that opinion. The client comes to the lawyer as an expert, implicitly trusting and accepting him as a guide and he should respond to this trust by thoroughly fitting himself to do his best. How many lawyers do this? Do not many take the statement of the client and their general knowledge of law as their guide and make an impromtu guess, nailing it down with the assurance that the client has a "good case" and is sure to succeed? Often indeed have men and women embarked in litigation upon assurances so formed and been led to their ruin.

In making assurances based upon such small information the lawyer is guilty of gross negligence, incompetency or positive dishonesty. Also, it is the duty of the lawyer to conduct his client's business with as little loss to the client as possible. He should not prolong it to increase his own compensation or that of his friends. He should not discourage a settlement when one is advisable. The interest of his client should be his compass. How many lawyers are there who observe this duty in its fullness? Perhaps not many prolong litigation to increase their own compensation, but more are not diligent in trying to settle the litigation that is profitable to them. Still more neglect preparation where the client is unable to pay for the work.

A lawyer should not charge an unreasonable fee. The client trusts the lawyer to determine the amount of services necessary to be rendered and to fix the price therefor. So intimate is this relation between attorney and client and so kindly disposed are clients toward their lawyers that they often submit to excessive charges without complaint.

Some lawyers take advantage of this trust; they exaggerate the importance of their services and exact excessive compensation where they think it will be borne by the client without strife. The self-interest of the attorney may lead him unconsciously to an inflated notion of his services, but the deliberate attempt of a lawyer to take advantage of the necessities of his client and thereby exact what the lawyer knows to be an unreasonable fee is as bad as burglary and seems worse, for it involves the betrayal of a sacred trust. It is like robbing an insane ward or plundering the estate which a dying man has left in one's possession.

Second: It is the duty of the lawyer to be honest with the court.

The judge depends upon the lawyers for his information. They should aid him by a fair and truthful presentation of the law and facts tending to support their respective sides; they should furnish him with such arguments as they believe will assist him in solving the difficult questions involved. If they fail to do this or strive to mislead him relative thereto, they make it less likely that he will come to a correct decision.

Some lawyers set traps and drag nets to cause the court to stumble, in order that the errors he is thus caused to make may be used on appeal to reverse the judgment. Some boast of their success in this regard. They accept employment on the wrong side when they behave or know their client is not entitled to any relief whatever and expect to be defeated on the trial. Then to gain time and baffle their adversary they induce the court to make mistakes and use these mistakes to get a new trial thereafter.

They thus violate their duty to the court and to the public and become obstructions in the administration of justice. The great zeal which every lawyer has for his client may cause him to exaggerate unconsciously, but the lawyer who intentionally deceives the judge either by false testimony or unfair citations from authorities or by arguments which he believes to be unsound can find no justification in conscience.

How many lawyers are entirely free from fault in this respect? Human nature is weak. The trial lawyer in the management of a great case where the fortune, liberty or life of his client is at stake is fired to such a white heat of zeal to win that it is very difficult for him to be perfectly honest, fair, frank, and truthful in his dealings with the court. Some very eminent law writers and judges have gone so far as to justify the undertaking of defenses which the advocate knows to be spurious.

It is said that the great Roman lawyer Cicero contended that the lawyer should be prepared to advocate either side with equal zeal and effect. This question opens a great field for discussion, and much may be said pro and con. The scope of this volume will not permit an extended disquisition, but the writer cannot bring himself to believe that any lawyer should ever advocate a proposition which he does not believe to be sound, or try to induce the court to render what he considers a false judgment.

In doing so he not only debases his own mind but if he succeeds, he pollutes the Fountain of Justice. Until the lawyer is convinced that the client has some rights under the law on the basis of truth he should not undertake his case and if at any stage of the proceedings he discovers that he has been misled in this particular he should withdraw and the cause be advocated if at all by someone who does believe it to be just. This might occasion some delay and inconvenience, but it would be far better than having a member of the legal profession become the dishonest advocate of and partner in a judicial crime.

[111]

Third: It is the duty of the lawyer not to deceive or mislead the jury.

These men often unlearned, inexperienced and impulsive are easier deceived and misled than the experienced judge. They are more responsive to appeals for sympathy or to prejudice. They may be swayed by sallies of wit or stampeded by furious denunciation and the trained orator having the last speech may cause them to forget the evidence, disregard the instructions of the court and decide the case upon his frantic appeal.

The peculiar susceptibility of this body to such influences makes it the duty of the lawyer to be particularly careful in what which he expects to win upon the law, and relies only on truthful evidence, there is no reason why he should not keep the minds of the jury clear from improper influences or any distracting matter. If he has not such a case, he should not appear at all. How frequently have lawyers erred in this respect?

In many cases tried before a jury the overzealous advocate has resorted to every device, he could employ for fanning the passions and prejudices of the jury and leading their minds away from the evidence and law as laid down by the court. He has tried to destroy the credit of the opposing party and his witnesses by unfair assaults upon their characters, inuendoes, sneers and sarcastic utterances and at the same time he has flattered the jury, courted their acquaintance, and striven by smiles and fawning to win their favor.

Many lawyers have thus vied with each other in their efforts to mislead the jury. This practice has been encouraged by the public. Lawyers who have attained the greatest skill in it have been held in the highest esteem and paid the largest compensation. They have been frequently employed in doubtful cases or those that have had no merit because it was believed that they could thus mislead the jury.

The literature of our nation contains many allusions to triumphs obtained this way. Histories and biographies of prominent lawyers parade the practice as worthy of emulation. But how, we ask in all sincerity, can a thinking mind justify such a practice which debases and perverts the administration of justice at its very fountain head and makes the trial of a case an uncertain farce depending upon dishonesty and deception instead of on a dignified and honest effort to arrive at the exact truth.

The lawyer who thus misuses his powers becomes debased to an extreme degree and after a few years' experience in this line becomes so accustomed to falsehood and dishonest advocacy that he no longer has any respect for the truth. He becomes a peddler of false wares, a trafficker in lies, a hired

[113]

slanderer, and the agent of any scoundrel who has enough money to pay him for his self-abasement.

Fourth: A lawyer should also be honest with his opponents.

A lawsuit is sometimes regarded like a dog fight governed by no rules of honor which either party is required to respect. This is a mistake. Even warfare has its code of honor. It is not considered proper to use poisoned bullets or to contrive the defeat of an enemy by counterfeiting its money, or by killing prisoners. No kind of combat between civilized persons is without some rules which neither party can transgress without disgrace.

The lawsuit is an intellectual battle, but it is a battle for justice. Who takes part in it should do so because he wishes justice? Justice has ever been considered by noble men as the most precious thing in all this world; so valuable that even life itself may be freely given to obtain it. In its name the greatest and the best have cheerfully become martyrs and gone to the gates of death as to a banquet. What then should be said of that villain who asserts that he is striving for justice and yet violates her precepts while engaged in the strife.

"Who seeks equity must do equity" is a maxim of the court of conscience, and it is certainly the duty of the lawyer to deal justly and fairly with his opponent. He may not disclose to him the sources of his strength. He may not strew flowers in his way, but he should not use false pretenses, trickery or deception to prevent him from fully and fairly presenting his side of the case. The lawyer who understands his case and believes it to be just has no need to use falsehood or chicanery and if he does, he unnecessarily stains what would otherwise be a clean record with corrupt matter and endangers his just cause by giving it a bad appearance.

No appeal is stronger than an appeal to conscience. So powerful is it that even rogues are moved by it, and just men listening to it catch glimpses of the divine image. A knave is flattered when his conscience is appealed to and thus is made friendly by the plea. Other things being equal the strongest lawyer before the court or jury from the Justice of the Peace to the nation's highest court is the one who makes the clearest show of good faith in behalf of himself and his client, from the inception to the conclusion of the case.

He never says or does a thing containing the slightest appearance of falsehood or unfairness to anyone; who treats the judge as if he had confidence in his intelligence and integrity; who treats the jury as if he expected them to justly and fairly discharge their duty. He treats the witnesses as if he desired them to tell the truth and was satisfied when they did; who treats his opponent as if he wished to give him a full opportunity to present all the facts and law on his side of the case.

[115]

Such a lawyer may occasionally lose, for such is the weakness of human institutions that even a just cause may be sometimes lost, and the just man after he has done his best to ascertain the truth may be mistaken in his judgment. But such an honest presentation will usually win; and win much oftener than any presentation encumbered with the appearance of unfairness or falsehood. But leaving out all questions of policy, a fair and truthful presentation is the only one that can be consistently tolerated in a court of justice.

If it is wrong for a plaintiff to try to collect a fraudulent claim, it is wrong for a defendant to present a spurious defense; if it is wrong for the parties themselves to seek to defraud each other and resort to the courts for that purpose it is equally wrong for a lawyer to aid either of them in such an attempt. An honest purpose may be assumed for a time and some be deceived by it, but this part cannot be so successfully acted as to long deceive many persons. There are rents in the garments of the false pretender which open despite him and constantly expose to the keen eye of the observer his real purpose.

Observe the advocate who has undertaken a cause which he knows to be unjust; note his proceedings from the inception to the conclusion of his case, and you will find, on every paper that he draws, the finger marks of his corrupt purpose. His claim or defense will be stated with undue verbosity. If for the plaintiff, his claim will be stated in many counts, setting forth the cause of action in different ways, making it uncertain what the real ground is. If for the defendant, he pleads many inconsistent pleas, most of which are manifestly false and fictitious.

During the trial he is constantly objecting and taking exceptions hoping to involve the record in error. His speeches are stuffed with pretenses of honesty and appeals to the jury to be fair to his "honest" client, to believe his "honest" witnesses, and thus by much protesting he strives to cover his fraudulent tracks until he has left hummocks over them.

He smiles, smirks, and plays the courtier; he struts, swaggers and bluffs; he besmears the opposing party and his witnesses with venomous matter, he decorates his own client and witnesses with angelic plumage. He affects great piety and calls upon Deity vociferously. He appeals for sympathy and makes an unseemly parade of what he claims to be the sufferings of his client. He scatters his argument and interjects all kinds of sophistry.

He tries to be witty and flowery. He seeks a personal controversy with the opposing attorney. He lugs into the record matters which have no bearing upon the case and from start to finish tries to cloud the atmosphere of the case with doubt, suspicion and confusion. Nor does he exhibit his corrupt purpose in the conduct of the case alone. You can see it in his wandering eye, you can detect it in his uneasy, shifting manner. Even the tone of his voice has a hollowness that tells the practiced ear that he is conscious of a criminal intent.

On the contrary, note the conduct of the lawyer who believes that he has a just cause and that the law and the facts will fully sustain it. Notice the direct manner with which he states his claim, or defense; how clear, few and exact the expressions which he uses. Without bluster or parade and at the proper time he states what he claims the facts to be, — not clouding with extravagant phraseology the plain facts of his statement nor concealing by pretenses of ignorance or lack of preparation the matters which he expects to prove.

Observe how ready he is to admit that which he knows to be true, how few are his objections and exceptions; how short and terse and to the point are his arguments; how free from rhetorical flourishes, attempts at wit, appeals to passion, or statements of flattery are his addresses to the court and jury. But more than all this, observe his personal appearance and the expression of his countenance.

He may not have the powerful form of Achilles; his brow may be wrinkled with the cares of anxious years; his eyes may lack luster from long years of study ; his shoulders may be stooped and shrunken; his form may be crippled by toil or disease, he may be physically as frail as consumption going downhill to the grave; but there will shine from his face a holy light, which will convince all who see it that an honest man has appealed to a court of his country to establish a just cause.

The wrongs of his client require no palaver, they are beetled upon his brow. His firm faith in the justice of his cause flashes from his eyes, and there is an invisible psychic power which comes from the very soul of things that drives his words into the hearts of men and wins them to his cause. An honest purpose is the essence of eloquence.

The lawyer should excel all other men in his love of truth and his enthusiasm for the right. No others are so closely allied with these as he and to no others is their importance made so apparent.

That the time will come when he will place them higher than all other considerations I firmly believe. The fact that he does not always do so now is an offspring of that erroneous supposition, that the lawyer is everybody's dog, who must respond to the call of any scoundrel whose misdeeds have placed his life or liberty in jeopardy.

A person charged with crime should be able to convince an honest lawyer that he has in truth legal rights, before any court is called upon to try them. If he cannot do this, he should plead for mercy to the pardoning power and not place upon the public the expense of conducting a trial wherein a guilty person by tricks and false pretenses is but trying to outwit the court into giving a false verdict.

CHAPTER XIV.
Physical and Spiritual Development

Physical development

Industry is becoming yearly more essential in the practice of the law. So many and complicated are the subjects which require investigation, so nice and exact the technical points to be decided, so numerous the decisions, statutes and constitutions that bear upon the questions in issue, so frequent the changes and modifications in the law, that the lawyer must of all men be the most active and alert. Many fail in this respect. Study and meditation tend to produce physical inactivity and cause the professional man to shrink from physical exertion and depend upon others to wait upon him until he accumulates much adipose tissue about his vital organs.

From this physical laziness comes a lack of mental energy and the lawyer thus afflicted settles into the rut where he can exist with the least exertion bodily and mentally. Thus, he inculcates the habit of acting upon mere impressions and intuitions and does most imperfect work. This condition comes partly from a false pride and dignity derived from ancient customs.

Those high in authority and those possessing riches have usually kept many servants ready to answer at call and obey their directions. The professional man who can afford it has imitated these habits and this has done much toward degenerating the individual. From it has come the notion that everyone should be a specialist prepared for some particular work and none other, so that even the poor in the most common departments of human industry assume a kind of rank or class out of which they are not willing to depart.

The legal profession has been afflicted with this folly. When lawyers to preserve their bodily health, find some physical activity necessary instead of exercising their bodies in the duties of their profession they often indulge in games and outdoor sports that are quite irrelevant. These give much relief. They often become so attached to these irrelevant sports as to seriously interfere with their professional duties. But some form of physical exercise is indispensable.

A descendant of a long line of idlers may inherit a physical structure which will enable him to exist in health and remain inactive, but American lawyers are usually the scions of physical strength. They have inherited bodies adapted to physical exertion and they cannot in one generation so

[122]

reverse the habits of their ancestors as to ignore the needs of the physical structure thus inherited and allow it to atrophy by disuse.

Our physical bodies are nourished and maintained only by reasonable use. This physical exertion must either be had in the discharge of the duties of the profession or be obtained in some extraneous, artificial, or irrelevant, practice. He will be the best lawyer who can combine physical and mental exercise in the discharge of the duties of his profession and has accumulated no false dignity which prevents him from doing anything that is necessary to be done.

He will keep his muscles free from excessive fat and ready for use and take delight in performing any useful service. By thus combining expert bodily activity with a keen and alert mind he becomes more than a match for any lawyer who must be waited on in everything and abstains from physical exertion until he is so fat, he has difficulty to move about.

To the man thus evenly developed, physical activity and mental exertion will be both a pleasure and his professional labor a delight, while the lawyer physically dormant will soon dread all exertion mental as well as physical and finally become so lazy that every duty will distress him. He will acquire fatty degeneration of the heart and a similar degeneration of the brain and finally become unfit for his professional duties.

Spiritual Development.

Surely none have greater need of spiritual development than the lawyer. He should be religious in the highest sense. By religion I mean a sincere consciousness of an obligation to the management of the universe which transcends all other ties; a conviction that conscious life is given as a trust to be discharged by working for the betterment of all, for the development and perfection of the whole according to one's highest ideal.

It is the militant spirit which regards birth as a call to arms in the Divine service, from which the faithful soldier will never be mustered out. This thought inspires the upward glance, unscales the eye of faith, produces that inflexible courage which remains undaunted under the most trying ordeals, and with prophetic eye sees beyond the mists of doubt and chance to the final triumph of the eternal right. This religion has been the inspiration and support of the greatest in all ages, the authors, poets, painters, soldiers, statesmen, philosophers and martyrs. But nowhere is it more useful than in the legal profession. Without it the well-trained lawyer will often give way under the disappointment and disaster that threatens to overwhelm him.

[124]

This religion may not make one conventional, nor scrupulous in ceremonial rites. A man may possess it and be profane. He may fail to observe any or all of the established religious practices of his time and country. He may not connect himself with any of the institutions for the propagation of religious doctrine. He may regard the creed of his fellow citizens as fallacious or absurd, and yet have a faith that gives strength to withstand the storms of misfortune, live for the benefit of humanity and die in the consciousness of duty well done. But it is better that the lawyer familiarize himself with the religious faith of his contemporaries, their customs, rites, and usages and if he cannot conscientiously practice them, he should not needlessly antagonize them or show them disrespect.

They appear true to his fellow citizens and adapted to their natures and are sacred in their eyes. As the wise traveler in foreign climes adopts so far as he may the wearing apparel, customs and manners of the people with whom he associates so will the wise lawyer facilitate his journey in his profession by conforming as far as he can consistently to the practices and customs of the society in which he moves. Of course, he must be honest, and cannot be a hypocrite without degradation. But most of the manners and customs of mankind are indifferent in moral significance. Their chief merit lies in the fact that they are established and thereby they constitute a part of the order of society.

Such for illustration is the custom of turning to the right in some countries and turning to the left in others. If both persons turn to the right they pass without collision, but if one turns to the right and the other to the left, they collide and obstruct each other. There is however no moral reason why it should not be as correct to turn in one direction as another, except that the structure of organized society requires some custom and the established one becomes the one necessary to be obeyed. By thus observing the established order, social life moves in music like a good dancer in the dance and the product is the happiness of all.

Many lawyers lack religion as here defined. They feel no obligation to promote the cause of righteousness. They stand ready to sacrifice the just rights of persons, communities, and even the government that they may wear the gaudy plumage of present riches. They will sell the liberties and even the lives of their fellow citizens and fashion shackles to torture millions yet unborn, if they can receive the golden drippings from such nefarious schemes. They will descend to depths of self-abasement almost beyond belief.

No greed besotted slave of Mammon ever had a scheme so vile, so desperate, so fraught with human woe, so deaf to decency and pity, that he could not find a lawyer, yes, some trained and learned member of the bar who would for a fee share in this infamous design. No talent, learning or skill, will make a righteous lawyer. That religion only will do it which puts the right above all other motives. This quality is the spiritual crown of the good man and whether he be a king upon a throne or a serf in a slave pen, if he has it, he has a great soul and can become an efficient worker anywhere. He is a solid plank in the ship of state. But if he has it not, he cannot be safely used in any place.

CHAPTER XV.
Some Common Errors

The Self-Reference Error

Examine the orations which have come down to us, political, religious, scholastic, or scientific and you will find them replete with references made by the speaker to himself, sometimes garrulous but usually in self-commendation. Go into the pulpit, the rostrum, or the legal forum and listen to the addresses of the most noted speakers and you will hear many such references.

One would suppose that a lawyer of experience who has an antagonist ready to expose and magnify his weak points would be less likely to indulge this practice than others, yet in every court in the land and even before the most august court in the nation, the battle-scarred veterans of the bar, speaking under a time limit in cases of the greatest importance, where every word is precious, introduce themselves in evidence and discuss their own personalities when attempting to discuss questions of law.

This practice sometimes crops out in printed briefs. Can there be any doubt of its folly? The personal character of the speaker, his likes and dislikes, the extent of his experience, his family or political relations, are entirely out of place. Is not all self-adulation odious and self-depreciation foolish? Do not these references unnecessarily consume the time of the court and distract the attention from the real points in question as well as weary the listener?

That lawyer will be the most effective who can rivet the attention of the court and jury to the pivotal question in the case and bring their attention in the clearest and best manner to the most convincing facts tending to establish his theory.

The Personal Abuse Error
Closely connected with the self-reference error is the practice of abusing the adversary. The lawyer who parades his own personality for emulation is almost certain to defame his adversary. Few indeed are the lawyers who argue cases without some scurrilous reference to the opposing lawyer and many include the opposite party and all his witnesses, unless perchance some witness has aided his side and then he substitutes fulsome flattery for scurrility.

The personal character of the opposing counsel is not germane to the discussion and all aspersions against the character of the opposite party and his witnesses not supported by the evidence can only excite prejudice and mislead a weak-minded judge or jury. They rarely accomplish their object and when they do are vicious to a high degree, and the attempt should always be considered as bad as an effort to bribe the jury. It is to be hoped the time will come when these twin relics of barbarism, laudation of self and defamation of opponents, will no longer disgrace the forum, when the mind of the advocate will be sufficiently trained to discuss the real questions without entangling them with venomous matter.

The Flattery Error

The use of flattery as a device for obtaining results is well-nigh universal. By tickling the vanity of the victim his intellect is put to sleep and he becomes an easy prey. The success of this device depends upon the susceptibility of the victim to such blandishments and the skill and judgment with which this form of sedative is applied.

In some degree most persons are subject to this influence, although all admit such comments should have no effect whatever in forming a judgment on any proposition of fact or law. Reference to the personality of the judicial officer, whether a Judge or juror, should therefore be considered offensive because irrelevant, and being used to take advantage of a supposed weakness is a reflection upon the intelligence of the officer. How frequently do lawyers of high standing and wide experience use this device when addressing Judges and jurors and how often are these tribunals cajoled thereby.

If the time shall ever come when persons shall have acquired such mental acuteness that they will consider the questions under discussion, and those only, good men will refrain from such devices and knaves will see the folly of them. Then we will no longer hear the public speaker begin his address by expressing his delight at meeting such an intelligent audience, the legislator will not refer to his "learned opponent," and the lawyer will not descant upon the integrity or intelligence of the jury or the learning and fairness of his Honor upon the bench.

Impassioned Eloquence Error

Since suitors have been represented by advocates it has been customary for these advocates to appeal to the feelings and passions of the court. The law student is often referred to the passionate orations of Grecian, Roman and English lawyers, as models of forensic eloquence. This way his youthful mind has acquired the idea that to become a great lawyer he must be a master of the art of "stirring men's blood."

When he begins his practice, he soon finds that his standing at the bar and with his client depends upon his capacity to make such appeals. There never was a time in a government of law when such appeals were truly in order. The English and American laws forbid the deciding of a case on account of passion or prejudice by either courts or juries and verdicts are often set aside when it appears that they have been so obtained. Jurors are charged to refrain from any sympathy with either party or bias in favor or against either side.

The surest means of reaching an accurate judgment is to keep the mind entirely free from any feelings in favor of or against either party. No person is ever assisted in forming a correct judgment by having his emotions harrowed up by passionate appeals. On the contrary, he is likely to be prevented from giving the matter an intelligent and impartial consideration. What the law is in a given case is a matter of fact which cannot be varied in the slightest degree by any passionate appeal.

What the truth is on any disputed point in the evidence is another fact which no amount of enthusiasm can alter. The only effect these oratorical pyrotechnics can have upon the decisions of law or disputed questions of fact is pernicious. Why then are they indulged in by able and conscientious lawyers? Why then are they permitted by the court? Why do the general public endorse such efforts? If jurors are not allowed to consider them why should lawyers be permitted to make them?

Before human government had crystallized into a system of positive law cases were decided upon public sentiment, or the notion the tribunal had of justice. Such appeals may have then been applicable as they are now applicable in legislative bodies where the law is being enacted or in appeals to the pardoning power, or to the judge when called upon to fix a sentence. But where the inquiry is merely what is the law and what are the facts such appeals have no place.

They are inconsistent with logic and the sound administration of legal justice and should be abandoned. The fact that such appeals are permitted and relied upon has greatly diminished the quantity of legal learning. Instead of diligently examining the decisions and statutes to ascertain the state of the law the advocate counts upon his capacity to befog the court and jury. He cudgels his imagination for pathetic and venomous matter and stuffs his mind in preparation for fireworks, hoping to dazzle his auditors, wring their hearts and drive them to his side by storms of indignation against his opponents.

He also neglects to investigate all the surrounding circumstances and to produce in evidence all the facts which tend to support his case, preferring to rely upon extraneous matter and the products of his imagination to procure a decision. There has been some progress in this practice for the better in recent years. The old-style orators are rapidly passing, and when the pernicious character of this rhetoric is fully realized the court may not be so interesting to onlookers, but it will come nearer giving accurate judgments.

The Boasting Error

Those who have taken part in contests of any kind requiring physical or mental excellence often waste much time in telling their experiences. The soldier who took part in a thrilling exploit in his youth may spend much of the remainder of his life in talking about this experience and thus his honorable action be made a great tax upon his energies for the balance of his days Travelers who have encountered a perilous journey and some who have had journeys consumed much of the time of their friends and acquaintances in telling over and over again what they have encountered. Persons who have held a prominent office frequently find it necessary afterwards to revert to the fact when it is immaterial to the subject under discussion.

The experiences of the lawyer ought to do much toward curbing this disposition. His training and acute knowledge of human nature should make him aware of its waste of time and annoyance to others and the bad taste thus exhibited. But does it? A large proportion of the ablest and best trained lawyers are guilty of this folly. Clients, friends, casual acquaintances and even persons just introduced are asked to listen to the details of victories in court, statements of shrewd plans laid, and smart things said, and applause gained. So common has this vice of boasting and self-laudation become among successful lawyers that but few persons enjoy their society.

It would not seem so bad if these blowers of their own horns would pause for a few moments and peacefully listen while the other fellow has a chance to blow his horn, but they become very uneasy and much distressed whenever anybody else attempts to indulge in the same practice. That is how they exhibit the common feelings of mankind, for people generally do not relish the boasting even of their friends. These emanations are either a species of cheap advertising or external manifestations of conceit and vainglory and they are usually unreliable.

It is generally known that the one who brags of his own exploits rarely tells the exact truth. The laudation of self is also oppressive upon the person who must listen, for he is under a constant strain to maintain his own individuality against the towering picture that the blowhard draws of himself and if he cannot do this he is depressed by a feeling of self-depreciation. Life is short even with the most fortunate and the brief time allotted ought to be used for some more

[135]

beneficent purpose than that of boasting or listening to someone else boast.

The wise person acts and lets the action speak for itself while he acts again trying to make each act more worthy of emulation than the one which preceded it. It is the foolish who having done something creditable make the fact of its performance a curse to themselves and humanity by forever afterwards advertising and exalting it.

The Error of Predicting Future Events

The prophet has always been abroad in the land. Where there is the least knowledge there is the greatest taste for prophecy. Future events ordinarily depend upon so many unknown causes that none can foretell what will happen to a certainty, and yet there are multitudes willing to pay for these guesses and rely upon them.

None know better than the lawyer how foolish it is to predict the result of a lawsuit; that all controversies depending upon the opinion of the court relative to questions of law or fact are always doubtful until the court of last resort has denied the petition for a rehearing. Yet there are many lawyers who predict results in lawsuits to their clients, the general public and to their friends.

In dealing with their antagonists they also hauntingly prophesy their own success. They quiet their own nerves, lull

[136]

their clients into inactivity and cause them to base their future transactions upon these predictions. When defeat comes these prophets collapse or become distracted and the client experiences a shock which disgusts him with the courts and prevents him from appealing the suit. If the lawyer instead of predicting success had properly explained the uncertainty of the result and thus prepared his client for disaster, the defeat would not have been such a catastrophe.

If the client had realized how much the result depended upon his own exertions, he would have made a greater effort in preparation and might have won. The lawyer deals with practical matters, the issue of which depends upon his wisdom, preparation, and skill in the management of his forces. He loses time and credit and wastes his energies when he assumes foreknowledge. He should leave the field of prophecy to clairvoyants, fortune tellers and mystics.

The Error of the Story-Telling Habit

It is usual to tell stories in public speeches. Even where the proposition is so plain that it needs no illustration, a story is often told for the pretended purpose of illustration. Some speakers have acquired renown as orators whose addresses were but a series of stories joined together with but slight connection, the stories being used not to illustrate the subject pretended to be discussed, but the subject itself a mere incident selected to accommodate the string of stories which are told. Where the object is entertainment and those entertained have no serious purpose, these stories aid in passing an idle hour, but in court where the time is precious and the business urgent, storytelling except in extreme cases is out of place.

Such stories are usually far-fetched, and generally fictitious and misleading and are intended to tickle the fancy and distract the attention, instead of instructing the mind. The teller of funny stories will usually draw a crowd who give but small attention to his subject. They think principally of the speaker and the stories they expect him to tell, and the speaker feels under bonds to be funny and smart to meet this expectation of his audience. He becomes self-conscious to a high degree and is prevented from making a close argument. The time during which any listener can concentrate his mind upon a subject is short. The minds of the best listeners are likely to wander after they have listened one hour. The majority are unable to endure the strain that long.

The advocate should avoid scattering and come at once to the pivotal point in the case, improving the moments when the Judge and jury are the most responsive. These moments are at the beginning of his address. He should reach the gist of the controversy quickly and avoid everything tending to distract attention and should hold his listeners to the subject under discussion. He should plainly and clearly present the facts and the reasons that support his theory. It is far better that his hearers adopt his views than that they think him an amusing orator on the wrong side.

Occasionally a startling incident may be used to fix a point in the minds of the jury. There are other places where the mind stocked with stories may display its exhibit.

Those who apply the practice of telling stories usually become addicted to it to an unreasonable degree.

Lawyers while in counsel with a client become garrulous, waste his time and their own and as age increases they become story telling bores repeating over and over again the same old yarns to the same person, and peddle familiar tales which have become a part of the folklore of the community.

The days when the practicing lawyer had time to tell stories for the amusement of the idle crowd in the courts, on the street corners, and in hotel lobbies and yet keep posted in his profession have passed away. If we knew more about the eminent men in the last generation who spent their time in that manner, we might find that they were not so learned in the law as their reputations would seem to indicate. In those days there were but few reports and treatises and they relied upon the light of nature, and the good will of the court and jury for success.

The profession now must use a great and ever-increasing library of authorities, statutes and scientific books. Lawyers are now likely to see justice many times miscarry if they do not become familiar with the books that treat upon the subjects in controversy. Loose, scattering remarks and long-winded tales must give way to accurate and precise statements supported by creditable evidence and authorities.

Errors in Gesticulation

The lawyer usually speaks "offhand" and uses both his hands, arms and sometimes his feet and legs in so doing. Sometimes he threshes the fleeing air with his clenched fists; at others he hammers the table in front of him until it groans with discomfort. Often, he clasps his hands together and chops the atmosphere between him and the jury, or separates his hands and swings his arms like flails, or works them as pump handles. Sometimes he may cause one hand to skim like a swallow while the other coquettishly caresses his coat tails.

Occasionally he bores the palm of his left hand with the index finger of his right or pounds the aforesaid palm with his clenched fist. He often shakes his head like an enraged bull fighting a red flag; or he paces back and forth before the jury, increasing his speed according to the rapidity of his utterances. All these and many other grotesque and absurd gestures are supposed to aid his argument in some way. But they do not. They are mere mannerisms which wear out his strength and tend to make him appear ridiculous.

They show that the speaker has lost, or is losing his head, that he has worked himself into an unnatural mental state which is expressing itself in these unusual antics and gyrations of his physical body.

Error in Using the Voice

Nor are the gestures employed by the jury lawyer more absurdly ridiculous than the tones of voice he uses when delivering his address. The jury are seldom more than a few feet from the speaker, often so near that they could hear him if he whispered, yet the lawyer sometimes talks so loudly that he can be heard for a block. Some of his methods of emphasis are to yell like an Indian, to scream like a screech owl, or to growl like a grizzly bear.

Sometimes he strikes the key of the donkey's bray, or whines like the mourning whang-doodle. At others he howls Uke a hound on a fox's trail. Sometimes he lifts his voice to the roof of his mouth and croons a lullaby and then lets it fall until it seems to issue forth from a cellar. Often a sing-song semi-quaver lulls the jury to momentary repose from which they are aroused by a rasping guttural squeak that grates upon their ears and nearly sets them crazy.

Many speakers soon after starting reach a monotone pitched about three notes above the ordinary talking key and hold the pitch without variation until the end of their address. This has a most soporific effect upon the court and jury and makes them wish for a bed where they might attain to a state of unconsciousness.

Few indeed are those who use common ordinary tones and depend solely upon the ideas conveyed for effect, yet such are the most sensible; they save their strength and get the best attention from those they address toward the subject they discuss. They certainly make a much better impression than those who stir themselves into a wild frenzy and exhaust the subject by exhausting themselves; whose excessive inspiration produces perspiration, until dripping like a drowned rat, they finish or rather collapse into a kind of nervous prostration.

The Objection Error

All who have witnessed many trials have been surprised by the practice among attorneys of making prolix, unnecessary and absurd objections. In most jurisdictions there is a rule of law requiring that an error in the decision of the court in admitting testimony cannot be urged on appeal unless an objection is made in the trial and has been overruled and an exception taken. The objection should be an expression of the opinion of the lawyer who makes it that the question or evidence is improper, and his exception should be his affirmation of that position after the court has ruled. Good faith on the part of the lawyer should prevent him from making untrue and unnecessary objections and from taking an improper exception.

Do the lawyers always show good faith toward the court when they fill the record of proceedings with great numbers of exceptions? Do they really believe that all the questions and evidence that they object to are improper in law and that the court is wrong in every instance where they take exceptions? If they do, they are unfamiliar with the most elementary rules of evidence. It seldom occurs that the Judge makes more than half a dozen mistakes in the trial of a case and in most cases these mistakes are not so many and yet, hundreds of objections and exceptions are often taken during a day's trial.

Also note the character of the objections. They usually state no grounds whatever, or else they state a great number of grounds most of which are manifestly absurd. Thus does the lawyer show a lack of preparation and understanding of the questions involved and a dense ignorance of the rules of evidence and thus he adopts a blunderbuss method of firing into the record every ground of objection he can imagine, hoping by luck or chance to hit something that may aid in getting a reversal of the judgment.

Where verbatim reports of the proceedings are taken and these are transcribed and made of record, these needless objections make much unnecessary expense to the parties. An advocate should know the rules of evidence, be prepared to make and urge specific objections, and feel himself in honor bound not to encumber the record with objections or exceptions that he has no good ground for urging.

The Cross Examination Error

Much of the time of the court is wasted by unnecessary cross examination. One party puts a witness on the stand and has him detail seriatim all the facts in his recollection, then the other party begins at the beginning of the witness' testimony and has him tell these facts all over again with such additions as may occur to him from further questioning. This is often done when the witness' testimony is not important.

The privilege of cross examination is accorded the other side to test the recollection of the witness, refresh his memory, impeach his credit by causing him to make inconsistent statements, and to bring out any other matter within the witness's knowledge pertaining to the subject that may assist the cross examiner.

Unless there is ground to suspect that the witness has testified falsely, there is no occasion to cross examine, unless it be suspected that the witness knows other facts which will aid the cross-examining party. Most cross examinations strengthen the testimony of the witness and emphasize it in the minds of the jury. It requires a very skillful cross examiner to expose a liar, especially if he is an intelligent one, and when this is done it is by outwitting him into admitting facts which tend to contradict him.

If such matter is pressed upon the witness, he usually extricates himself from the tangle. The contradiction of a false witness is thus accomplished if at all by a few questions. A lawyer sometimes attempts to break down a witness by a protracted cross examination conducted in an offensive manner and pushed with great rapidity.

This sweat-box process is more likely to confuse the truthful witness than the liar and it ought not to be permitted unless in very rare cases where there is something in the manner of the witness or his evidence which gives grounds for suspecting that his testimony is intentionally false. Persons forced to go to court as witnesses are entitled to decent respect, and treatment worthy of the citizens of a free country.

The witness is nobody's cur to be kicked and cuffed about by overzealous lawyers and should in every instance be given a fair chance to tell the truth as he remembers it. When he has told it, he should not be brow-beaten and insulted for the purpose of intimidating and confusing him. The fact that a liar may sometimes be compelled to tell the truth by this means cannot justify the abuse of everybody. The cross examination should be sensible, courteous, and limited to the necessary requirement of a decent and orderly administration of justice. This would greatly shorten the length of the trial, reduce the expense incurred and tend to create an atmosphere favorable to a just decision.

The Repetition Error

From a remote antiquity the practice has been prevalent of repeating either the same word or words expressing the same meaning for the purpose of emphasis. This practice may have been useful when the human mind was so feeble that it could not grasp an idea by hearing it once stated, or when the mere use of words mustered in formidable array had a thrilling effect without regard to their meaning.

In the practice of law we would expect to find less of this unnecessary use of words than elsewhere, because it is a learned profession and many of the words are the names of battle grounds wherein they have acquired a definite significance, and the lawyer's training should make him able to appreciate accurate distinctions. On the contrary there is no department of human learning where repetitions are more common than in the preparation of legal documents, pleadings, objections and speeches of lawyers.

[146]

An illustration is not necessary because there is scarcely a document, speech or pleading that can be referred to from the preparation of a common deed, lease or will, to the delivery of an opinion of the Supreme Court of the United States wherein this practice of repetition is not indulged.

This unnecessary verbosity coupled with the use of ponderous and uncommon words to express commonplace ideas seems to brand the profession with a lack of precision, or a deliberate desire to hoo-doo the ignorant and unthinking by a kind of incantation or rigmarole of high-sounding words. May we not hope for a day to dawn when the facts necessary to be stated in legal proceedings will be set forth in simple, clear and concise language, and all documents be so prepared as to be easily understood by everyone with none of that padding and unnecessary verbiage which serves no useful purpose and tends to confuse and increase the cost of placing them on the records?

CHAPTER XVI. A Foil

THE foregoing is not a complete list of the common errors prevalent in our profession. Every reader will be able to add to it and perhaps suggest characters more entitled to consideration than any herein sketched. The limit which the writer planned for this volume has been reached and the reader is probably weary of considering foibles and wishes to read something creditable to the profession. The delineation of the virtues and good qualities which are common at the bar would be a much pleasanter task to the author, but it does not properly belong to the subject, and would probably require a much larger book.

Merely as a foil to what has heretofore been written we take pleasure in presenting another character.

Lycurgus Law

Amid the barren mountains of a coal mining region a babe was born. His birth was considered a calamity, for his parents were very poor and were long past their prime. They had already raised six children all of whom had turned out badly.

Father had no education nor any respect for anyone else who had. He took pride in the fact that he could neither read nor write. Most of his life had been spent in the mines surrounded by dirt and danger, and it was more important for him to endure the cramped posture in which he toiled and accustom his lungs to the powder gases and coal dust than his eyes to the form of letters.

The mother however could read and did not share with her spouse his hatred for all book learning. She had taught their children to read in their infancy and might have done more in this respect had she not become afflicted with chronic dyspepsia and nervous prostration long before Lycurgus was born. The babe inherited a tendency to his mother's diseases, had nervous fits in his infancy, and suffered much from indigestion. The mother taught him his letters and how to spell before he was five years of age, and on his fifth birthday he started to school.

The next day a snowstorm came and be being barefooted, and his parents lacking the money to provide him with shoes his school days were over. Before the spring came, he had grown large enough to help his mother around the house, and he could not be spared to attend school. So, he remained at home until he was twelve. Then he began working with his father in the mine, and until he reached his maturity was engaged in the hardest and most offensive manual labor connected with the digging of coal.

Somewhere in the current of his life's stream coming down from a remote ancestry, there had fallen a seed which was destined to reach the light, and it had lodged in the brain of this child of poverty. Here in the darkness it struggled to burst the fetters of its hard conditions. Late at night, and in the early morning, and at every opportunity this boy eagerly read whatever books he could borrow. His father was much displeased by these habits and often expressed his displeasure in offensive epithets, but finding his opposition useless, pronounced the lad crazy and said no more.

The family lived in a Swedish settlement and the boy borrowed from the people a Swedish Bible and by comparing that with an English one learned many words in the Swedish language and was soon able to converse with the Swedish settlers in their own tongue. One of the laborers, who could speak no English had worked for an employer who refused to pay him for his work. This laborer laid his grievances before young Lycurgus and asked his assistance.

This youth of fourteen years ascertained by inquiries that there was such a thing as a Justice Court. There he went and brought the suit. This was his first case. Barefooted, hatless, clad in a ragged shirt and trousers, but strong with the courage which comes to the promoters of a just cause, he went into court, acted as counsellor, lawyer and interpreter, and succeeded in getting justice for his client.

[150]

Against him was pitted a lawyer of large experience, who made the best defense he could, claiming that there was no contract and the law created no obligation to pay for the services. But the magistrate maintained that law was justice and that it was not just for one man to refuse to pay another for his work.

This was the turning point in the lad's career. Suddenly his eyes were opened to the fact that there was a law which gave the poorest and feeblest protection against the richest and strongest. He began to enquire what that law was and how it came into being.

At a considerable distance from where he lived was a circulating library. To this he often journeyed on foot and borrowed books of history. He became familiar with the annals of his own country, of England, and many other nations. He learned that the body of our laws was a mighty temple, every stone in which had been hewn by generations of toil and cemented in its place by the blood of the bravest and best.

He became familiar with the choice spirits who had laid its foundation and he traced the growth of its splendid superstructure. He felt his bosom swell and his eyes filled with tears as he read of those who had put its mighty pillars in place. Sweet indeed was the message which came from

Runnymede when the great Barons of Britain forced the Magna Charta from King John, and set a boundary to the tide of despotism; but sweeter still the story of that day in Independence Hall, when the master minds of the American Colonies gave birth to a new nation, declaring in matchless eloquence the soul-stirring truths of human liberty.

He read again and again "Crisis" by Thomas Paine ;he read and reread Patrick Henry's immortal words in the Virginia Assembly; he was with Warren at Bunker Hill, with Washington at Valley Forge ; he scanned the long line of unnumbered graves that reaches far back in the remote past and connects the heroes of Thermopylae with the latest martyr for human rights. And notwithstanding the denunciations of the government heard about him, he learned to love the institutions of his country and reverence her flag, and he desired greatly to enlist in her service, by joining that body of men who have ever been the foremost to defend her in war, and to preserve her in peace.

This ambition to be a lawyer took full possession of his very soul. He was not particular where he began or who were his instructors, nor the standing of the school in which he was taught. He read all the law books he could get, he asked questions of any who would answer, and his school room was a fence corner or the dump at the mine.

Learning is a kind goddess: She always comes to those who seek her with a consecrated heart. She gives the pauper in the wretched hut as warm a welcome as the prince in his marble palace. In this manner was the youth of Lycurgus spent. He used no nervous stimulants. He contracted no debts he could not pay. He played no games. He sought no company among the gay. He guarded well his health and strength, that he might endure the work he had chosen. Finally, he entered a lawyer's office and later was admitted to the bar.

There for forty years he toiled as a lawyer, beginning at the bottom and rising among his fellows like some tall mountain laved by the ocean round its base which slowly rises as the waters wane. On the enduring granite of truth and justice he founded the citadel of his fame. He took no causes that were corrupt. No villain plea did ever pass his lips. He stood for no false doctrine if he knew it. No gold could buy from him a sham opinion. Compared with that rich jewel which his soul possessed of reverence for the just and true, all worldly wealth he thought but dross, all fame bought with debasement merely poisonous vapor.

He became a lawyer of the highest type. He knew the law, loved, and obeyed it. Not as a fetish but as a priceless legacy, to be valued for what it cost, guarded with zealous care, and only changed to make it better. He kept no trumpet blowing to tell his merits. He let his work speak for itself, content to do the best he could with that which came to him. He ordered all his work so that none would be neglected, and if he could not promptly try a case, he did not take it. He gave no preference to the rich above the poor, nor one above another, except the wrong that needed most to be redressed he gave his first attention. He kept the latest books and read the latest cases and was the first to learn of any change in law or doctrine. His office was kept in order and all his papers where they could be quickly found.

He was not called an orator, for what he said, not how he said it, claimed the most attention. He took no time to boast of what he did but kept on doing, striving each day to excel the day before. In every court, the lowest to the highest he went to plead his clients' causes. Judges and juries, committeemen and boards all heard him gladly.

They sought for light and what he said shed light upon the points in issue. Treating all with gentle courtesy he never flattered, nor did he like a suppliant beg for justice. He stood erect, a man, favoring on none, yet modestly he spoke the simple truth, most eloquent when told in clearest phrase. He did not wander from the issue, nor magnify with ponderous verbiage the wrongs he would redress, nor claim all virtue was his client's, or all vice dwelt upon the other side.

Nor did he speak in vain. Each victory brought him greater credit for probity and lore. Many when they saw him take the other side were warned thereby their case was well-nigh hopeless and by a careful re-examination found it so and quit the contest. Sometimes great questions, intricate and close, on which vast interests hung, not only for the present but all future time, arose and asked his aid. Then he before the nation's slightest court, his audience the world, made such an argument for human rights, that countless millions waited for his words. They came not forth in thunder tones; no lightnings rent the feverish air. But calm and clear and unabashed his arguments were made, and thus without a seeming strain he spoke the burden of this mighty task, as simply as some shepherd's tale.

Like some pure spirit from a better land, he came to talk to those who would do right and clearly showed the way.

His frequent winnings brought him great renown, and many suitors sought him in their cases, but most his fame spread as a counsellor. His associates at the bar made him their oracle, and to his office thronged to get his judgment. Judges descended from their stools to beg for his advice, and when their way was dark amid the quirks and quibbles of the books he pointed to the star of right and made the path to justice clear. Legislatures would often ask his judgment. For he knew the constitutions of the states and of the nation, had traced

[155]

their origin through all the battles that were fought about them and nearer than any other man could tell the meaning likely to prevail.

He held no office and yet the president and congress passed by their salaried aids and asked for his opinion, preferring to base the fabric of the law upon his judgment, then on their own. Ambassadors from foreign courts came to his office to get his counsel.

Once when a question in the laws of Nations threatened war, a mighty empire acted on his judgment. He saw the race for wealth but joined not in the chase; he heard fame's bugle blow for those whose lives were bad; he envied not their triumphs or renown; the siren song of sensual pleasure wooed his ear; he sought a higher joy. On every hand some pleasant voice called him to come and play; his heart was with his books and in that task, the noblest man has planned, he found sufficient to employ his time. Thus, did he live and work till death came like an evening zephyr and he died as gently as the clock runs down.

He built no marble palace to preserve his name, no granite temple now protects his dust. But firmer far than marble, granite or enduring brass, the strong foundation of his fame. As long as justice is adored, the principles he toiled for and established, shall be his monument, and those who read the simple story of his life shall feel new inspiration for the eternal right. As when the orb of day passes behind the western hills and leaves upon the heavens his fairest hues, so this grand soul passed in his progress onward far beyond the circle of our mortal vision, yet left a radiance filling all the land.

The world is full of work and ways for man to shine. War has its heroes, and when their cause is just, then glory's chaplets fitly mark their tombs. Bards may compete for fame and if their lines bear messages of truth and right they well deserve their bays. Riches may bring renown, when justly won and fairly used, and hard-earned gold may keep fame's taper burning when no breath of shame may rise to blow it out. But be the bid for laurels what it may, if anywhere it wears the stain of crime, the future will reject it. If this is true and so it surely is, then how can any lawyer hope to win the highest, richest prizes of the world and use his gifts for an ignoble purpose?

CHAPTER XVII.
The Nation's Need

Knowledge of law is one of the nation's greatest needs. Liberty in society cannot exist without laws embodying principles of equality and justice, and an authority strong enough to enforce those laws against all transgressors. A government based upon the popular will must be supported by people who understand and appreciate this and who will select representatives familiar with the principles of these laws and qualified to so change and fashion them that they may conform to the changing needs of the people.

Every citizen should therefore understand the constitution of his state and nation and have a general knowledge of the nature, scope and principles of the laws in force therein. Certainly no one should be considered educated who has not this knowledge, for without it he is not able to properly discharge his duty either as a citizen or an officer of his country. Knowledge of law is especially necessary to the members of all legislative bodies from the City Council and local boards to the Congress of the United States.

It is necessary in all important executive offices from the constable to the president and his cabinet and it is absolutely indispensable to the occupants of all judicial offices, and in those who assume to practice law. The pathetic fact is that not only the general public and their representatives in the government but even lawyers and Judges are sadly deficient in this knowledge.

There are many occupying inferior judicial offices who have never read the constitution of their state or of the United States, and probably could not find either in print, without the aid of a detective, or when found understand it without an interpreter. There are lawyers, many of them, who have probably not looked at these venerable documents since leaving school and at that time had no clear conception of their meaning. The statutes of their own state, they have never attempted to read, nor to acquire any general knowledge of them.

What knowledge they possess they have obtained by looking at the index for any subject on which a question has arisen and then following the lead of this index, for a brief glimpse at the sections referred to therein.

A few chapters may frequently have been looked at until quite familiar, but the rest has remained a sealed book. Many Judges are likewise deficient in knowledge of the written and fundamental laws of their country. Some of them in the highest courts do not even remember the decisions written by themselves and announce a contrary doctrine without being conscious of reversing their own decisions.

These mistakes of course happen only where the lawyers have neglected to look up and call the Judges' attention to their former decisions. So deficient are many lawyers and some Judges in knowledge of law and the books concerning it, that they are unable to find the law when the books are placed before them.

They are such strangers to these books and the manner of their construction, and so ignorant of the catch words used in the indices that they cannot without spending much time in examination find the text which treats upon the subject. Nowhere is ignorance of law more painfully apparent than in court trials, when an ignorant Judge and two or three ignorant lawyers are making an effort to play a game, the rules of which are unknown to them or where one lawyer familiar with the law is putting forth a spurious defense and shows no disposition to enlighten the bewildered Judge or the opposing counsel.

Many trial lawyers confine their practice to a certain line of cases such as the prosecution or defense of personal injury suits and do not assume knowledge of law outside of their specialty. Often these specialists gravitate into a rut, where they traffic in a few stock notions of the law and in their addresses use a collection of stock arguments which they string together like the provisions in a blank insurance policy filling in the names of the parties and witnesses as the occasion requires. These make no progress in legal learning and appear as ignorant as babies when a point is raised outside of the draught of their familiar blank.

Why then is the legal profession thus deficient in the knowledge of the law? Is it so difficult to obtain that only a person of transcendent intellect can procure it? It is not. Any person of ordinary intelligence with a fair knowledge of the English language and surely one with a preliminary legal education can without an instructor, by studying diligently three hours each day for five years become familiar with all important legal principles and the books in which they are contained. And after he has obtained this knowledge, he can retain it and keep familiar with the changes by spending one hour each day in an effort to do so.

The revised Statutes of Illinois including the constitutions of the state and nation and all the statutes in force in the state contains about 2,000 pages. A slow reader, reading three hours a day could read the book seriatim in less than three weeks, and a rapid reader could become familiar with its contents in one week.

The Second Edition of the American and English Encyclopedia of Law contains twenty-nine volumes of about 1,000 pages each. These pages embody the whole common law, and by reading three hours a day, a slow reader could read the entire twenty-nine volumes in less than a year, and a rapid reader could become familiar with them in half that time.

Then add to this reading a work of 1000 pages on the rules and forms of pleading in force in the state where the lawyer resides. This he could read in two weeks. He has now covered the whole field of jurisprudence and has at least three and one-half years out of the five left to review and reread and to read such other legal works as he may desire. This would seem ample.

The task of becoming familiar with the laws of one's country is not so great as learning to play well on the piano or violin and it does not require unusual talent. Why then do lawyers find it so difficult? It is because they dislike the task and make no systematic effort to discharge it.

They lack appreciation for their country's institutions. Its laws are dry and uninteresting to them and their minds recoil from such study. Their hearts are elsewhere. They have entered the profession to keep the wolf from the door and when they no longer hear him howl, they go to sleep or go to a banquet.

The average lawyer in the city gets to his office at some time between nine o'clock and nine-thirty in the morning. He looks at the newspapers, answers or makes a few telephone calls, and when not called to court has a few interviews with clients or visitors, dictates a few letters, and then it is lunch time. After lunch he returns to the office, has more interviews in person or by telephone, perhaps may work an hour or so on a pleading or argument, reads and answers more letters, pays or staves off his creditors and at four o'clock or four-thirty starts for his home or his club.

If he reads in the evening it is the newspapers, magazines or works of fiction. If he goes out it is to a club, lodge or card party from which he returns about midnight or later. Thus, the routine continues, until vacation; then, if he is able, he goes to Europe, to the mountains or to the sea.

During the year he may have tried a few cases and perhaps spent a few hours each day for several days in preparing to argue law questions arising in these cases; but with that exception his books except the statutes and digests which he must occasionally consult have remained upon their shelves, unless taken down to be dusted. In other words, the time he has spent in ascertaining the law has been determined by accident and its quantity has been as small as he could well make it.

With such habits he never becomes sufficiently familiar with his books to make a thorough brief and yet if prudent he usually succeeds in acquiring a competence financially. This has been his chief aim from the first and so he has succeeded.

The need of the nation is a well-educated bar whose members have a higher object than mere personal gain; who strive to make themselves familiar with its laws and with the principles of justice that underlie them; who themselves obey these laws and help to enforce them, and who will assist in securing such additions thereto and alterations thereof as will advance the common good and make the foundations of civil liberty stronger and wider. Not only the young man just entering the profession should realize this; but the old practitioner sixty years of age, forty-five years of which have been spent at the bar, still has an opportunity to become a thorough lawyer and render his country some service.

Seven hours a day spent diligently in legal study and work will in a few years make out of a common man a great lawyer and at the same time bring in enough money to support a sensible family and lay a foundation for age or misfortune. But these hours must be hours of concentrated attention when the mind is at its best and has no other object. Four or five of these hours should be in the early part of the day.

Having thus diligently worked and studied seven hours the remainder of the seventeen may be spent as the lawyer thinks best, providing of course he gets the rest necessary to fit him for his next day's task. It will allow him an abundance of time for enjoying all the exercises, recreations, and amusements to which his tastes incline and as much outside reading as he may relish. But proficiency in the law must be his paramount object, the idol to which he devotedly kneels. The administration of justice should be the absorbing desire of his soul. A firm faith in the final triumph of the right his inflexible support; the authority of the right to control all his actions an ever-recognized truth.

The wanderer in the wilderness may lose his way and then confused may seek the highest point where spreading out before his gaze the greatest area of the earth appears, and widest stretch of heaven is seen. Here he may find his way again and turn his wandering footsteps home.

The lawyer midst his labyrinth of cares pulled by the strings of many motives, surrounded by the howling wolves of greed, stung by the hornets of ingratitude, may stumble from his path and lose his way, proceeding recklessly till some deep gorge yawns threateningly before him. Then he should seek

[165]

the highest point, the loftiest motive that his mind can frame and scan the largest area of both earth and heaven, the paths behind over which through countless years the multitudes have passed, the paths in front that lead in divers ways and then with prudent care select the route that leads securely home. Before I bring this volume to its close, wherein I've tried to chart the pitfalls, chasms and poisonous swamps that lurk along a lawyer's way, I wish to turn the public's gaze toward a threatening tempest which I think approaches and speak a word to those who may be clients.

Our liberties, our property and our lives, all that we have and cherish most depend as I have shown upon a government of law. This government can never thrive save by the aid of lawyers who may know the law, nor be kept pure unless these lawyers strive to keep it so. The money-getting, soul-corroding vice may breathe its poisonous breath upon the press and fill the world with lies. The people may read but disregard and firm the nation stand. The pulpit too may drink its rank contagion and deck the rottenness of crime with flowers and yet no serious wreck come to the " Ship of State."

Doctors of medicine may take its virus and stand with keen edged knives ready to amputate the patient for his purse and many be untimely slain; the firm foundation of our mighty fabric remains unshaken. But should this hateful monster seize the bar, palsy the conscience that now loves the right, shrivel the hearts that now for justice throb, make minds that once were quick to keep the nation strong, as swift to make their countrymen their prey, what then awaits but ruin? What fate awaits the ship when those who have command conspire to sink it? Chaos will come and human rights be merely froth upon a raging sea. More than on armies, armaments, forts or battleships, the nation now depends upon the bar.

Its members are the nation's leading men in every walk of life. They are its legislators, courts and cabinets, and hold the reins in every lofty place.

Every young lawyer passing from the school to take his place among the legal ranks deserves consideration. If he be clean and honest and strives to do his best, give him a chance to serve you in an honest way. He may be bashful, backward and assume but little, may boast no noble lineage, and wear no heritage of fame; he may be poor, possess no library that he can call his own, and have no office which he can command and yet give you much better service in some cases than the hero of a thousand suits in whose fine office clients swarm and wait.

 Let not the glare of notoriety draw you into the blaze. Be not mislead by boasting in or out of print. High-minded, honest lawyers scorn to boast, employ no boosters, make no false pretense, nor scramble with indecent haste for gold. They may be poor and not in search of wealth and yet industrious and rich in learning and give you better service than any of the brood that does the crowing. Give honest worth a chance wherever you find it and thereby will you help to keep it honest.

If you instead go to the one who makes the loudest noise and has the least regard for right, and add your ingots to the largest pile, and turn from him whose honest and high minded zeal aspires without display to aid the true and just, then do you add the might of your strong arm to

break the firmest pillar that sustains the state. If all men do the like, the time must come when strife for gold will be the lawyer's only aim; when every scoundrel that designs a crime will use the law to aid in its committal and never fail to find, both at the bar and on the bench, those ready to assist and share the spoils; when legal lore will be a shield to help the thief and nerve the robber's arm, and every fund gathered by taxes to support the state will be a loot for lawyers and the pals.

Honor will sit no more upon the bench or plead for justice at the bar, and in its name the crafty will but smile while they contrive to pick your pockets. A government of law will then become a name to cloak corruption in its rankest form and hold its festering place till the disgusted, plundered, frenzied multitude arise by force and wipe it from the map.

And you, my brothers at the bar, raise high the standard of professional honor. Resist all efforts made to pull it down. Force to the rear all those who would debase it and strive for legal learning as a priceless gem. By doing thus you serve your country best, your children and yourselves, and pay in part the debt you owe to Providence who gave us this inheritance of liberty and law.

The Constitution is the stay that holds the nation's parts in place. Who would protect it, if you desert it? An honest, learned, and patriotic Judge must guard our liberties in every court. Unless you furnish such, where can that Judge be found? On your own shoulders now the burden lies. You cannot, must not, shirk it if you would.

The noblest fabric on the earth is in your hands. It is more precious than the wealth of all the world. The wretched everywhere look to its flag, as freedom's star. Its glorious colors make their bosoms swell with hope to break their bonds. If you are true and do not falter from the right, but ever for the just raise your strong voices, the tide of liberty, now rising everywhere, shall never ebb, but pushing onward with increasing force, flow to the farthest shore.

www.ingramcontent.com/pod-product-compliance
Lightning Source LLC
Chambersburg PA
CBHW021411210526
45463CB00001B/324